Traveling Home

Tracking Your Way through the Spiritual Wilderness

Mark R. Kowalewski

CHURCH
PUBLISHING
INCORPORATED

Church Publishing
19 East 34th Street
New York, NY 10016
www.churchpublishing.org

Cover design by Jennifer Kopec, 2Pug Design
Typeset by PerfecType, Nashville, Tennessee

A record of this book is available from the Library of Congress.

ISBN-13: 978-1-64065-194-4 (pbk.)
ISBN-13: 978-1-64065-195-1 (ebook)

CONTENTS

PREFACE

America in the early twenty-first century is an anxious place. We tend to distrust civic, cultural, and religious institutions. Apocalyptic language and mythic imagery appear seemingly everywhere. It seems that we need some basic foundation to ground our lives, to give us a sense of direction in the face of anxiety—not as a means of covering over fears, but as a way of finding true faith, hope, and, yes, even love in our society.

I believe an honest and thoughtful exploration of a spiritual path can provide such a firm foundation; the way forged by Jesus of Nazareth provides the direction for my life. The purpose of this book is to help you explore your spiritual journey by way of an ancient map created by the prophets, poets, and mystics in ancient Israel, and by Jesus himself and his disciples after him. At the same time, I know that the language of faith has been both co-opted as a political strategy and largely lost to our contemporary culture. The very words that may have guided generations past in both civic and religious discourse now hold meanings contrary to the message of Jesus or mean nothing at all when proclaimed in our churches. Even more troubling is that the very language of caring, compassion, and mutual respect embedded in the vocabulary of faith is disappearing from our public discourse, as Jonathan Merritt observes.[1] In the pages that follow, we will work to revive and reimagine the sacred words and landscape that can lead us to a vision of a better hope for our futures personally and globally.

---

1. Merritt, *Learning to Speak God.*

This book is meant for spiritual seekers. You may have been raised in a church or with a spiritual background. If that's the case, you may have certain preconceptions you want to explore about the faith in which you were raised. You may have had no spiritual background. In that case, I invite you to discover a new language and meet the God of the Bible. You may be coming back to church, or just discovering one, or maybe you are on the fence—standing spiritually in the "narthex," that lobby many churches have before you actually enter the sanctuary. While you can read this book on your own, it might be best to read it in a group of people. If you are part of a church, you may have been asked to read this book as a part of an exploration of Christianity. Maybe you have friends who are asking similar questions about faith. This book is a map to set you on course.

I believe the language of faith is best understood in poetry, music, and story, rather than the language of empirical investigation and analysis. Throughout what follows, I invite you to savor the stories and the poetry you will find as part of these pages. Allow your heart, as well as your mind, to engage the questions you may have.

I need to acknowledge some of the people who have helped me on my journey of faith and in writing this book. First, thanks to my editor Milton Brasher-Cunningham and the staff of Church Publishing for taking this project on. Also my profound thanks to all the spiritual seekers who for the past years have joined our Basic Christian Formation Class at St. John's Cathedral in Los Angeles. It is from that experience that this book emerged. I give thanks for the whole community of St. John's for making it possible for me to write this book and for the experience of Christians in community they have provided.

My brother Paul and sister-in-law Karen Kowalewski opened the doors of their desert retreat to me. It is here I have found time and space for solitary reflection. I had the privilege of completing much of the final manuscript under their roof.

The Rev. (now Bishop) Thomas Brown and the Rev. Thomas Mousin have provided me with untold hospitality in their home and in the magical place that is Thousand Islands, New York. I'm so grateful also for their invitation to join them on pilgrimage to the Holy Land where much of an earlier draft of this book was composed.

Finally, my greatest thanks goes to the members of my household who day in and day out provide the context for my daily Christian journey; to our dogs Ella, Jaimie, and Mr. Jack; but especially to Walter Killmer and his husband Daniel Ade, who is also my partner in ministry and whose ongoing support and encouragement continue to sustain me as we help God's garden grow.

1

Polaris

We had the sky up there, all speckled with stars, and we used to lay on our backs and look up at them, and discuss about whether they was made or only just happened.
—Mark Twain, *The Adventures of Huckleberry Finn*

Almost without a sound, a small ragtag group of men, women, and children make their way through the woods on a cold, cloudless night. Up ahead, one tall woman looks up into the moonless sky to search out the Drinking Gourd, the constellation pointing to Polaris, the North Star. They call the woman Moses, because she leads this group of escaping slaves through the Underground Railroad, guided by the light of the star that leads north to freedom and a new promised land.

Araminta Ross was born in Dorchester County, Maryland, in 1820. She began her life as a slave and later took the name by which we know her today—Harriet Tubman. In 1849, Harriet fled north and escaped slavery. The next year she returned to Maryland to help more enslaved people find their way to freedom. The woman they called Moses made nineteen trips and helped some three hundred slaves escape by means of the Underground Railroad. She traveled using backroads, and she moved often under cover of darkness, guided by the North Star.

You can always find Polaris in the Northern Hemisphere at any time of the year. The constellation the slaves called the Drinking Gourd and we know as the Big Dipper points directly to the pole star—always north. It is one star in the sky you can count on to find direction. It helped Harriet Tubman and the hundreds of people she helped on the Underground Railroad—and she never lost a passenger.

My good friends Thomas and Tom have a cottage in Thousand Islands in the St. Lawrence Seaway between New York State and Canada. A few summers ago, after having dinner at a home on one of the many islands that dot the river, we joined our friend Andrew, an expert boatman, who piloted us back to the cottage. He steered effortlessly through the waters—he had spent nearly every summer of his life on the river. When he was a boy, he and his brother would lie on the deck of their boat and look up at the night sky to find their direction using the stars. Years of experience taught Andrew how to navigate at night, how to avoid the shoals without a chart.

A strange sight appeared on that same St. Lawrence River in the summer of 2016. A Hawaiian canoe called the *Hōkūleʻa* traversed its waters on a voyage around the globe that began in 2013. The crew navigated the way their ancestors did, using the stars, the patterns of waves, the clouds, and even the flights of birds to find their way across the world. Nainoa Thompson, who planned the world tour, described the wisdom of this way of navigating in intuitive terms: "You only know where you are by memorizing where you come from."[1]

Most of us in the modern Western world find our way using a GPS. My phone has at least three separate navigation apps where I simply have to say or type in my destination and a voice tells me where to turn next. We can even find out where the next traffic jam is and where to turn to

---

1. If you want to know more about the history and voyage of the *Hōkūleʻa*, visit hokulea.com.

take the fastest route. Technology leads us to where we want to go. But where is that?

Finding Our Way

Boating charts, compasses, GPSs, guides, clouds, or the hundreds of stars that led ancient navigators can all lead us to physical places and help us not get lost. Yet a question still remains: how do we navigate the world around us—not so much in finding our way from point A to point B, but in a larger sense?

When a group of Hawaiians built the Hōkūle'a and sailed off to Tahiti they weren't just building a boat to get to a destination. They had a larger purpose and a greater desire. They sought to set their own experience in a larger story and recover ancient ways of navigating nearly lost for six hundred years. While they learned ancient practices of building and navigation, they sought to find a bigger picture, to recover a deeper identity, a sense of grounding for who they were reflected in the way they described the art of navigating: "You only know where you are by memorizing where you come from."

The same can be said for the people Harriet Tubman brought out of slavery. When she looked up at the Drinking Gourd and followed Polaris, north was not only a direction, it was a symbol of longing for a new place, a new life, a better hope, and the promise of tomorrow. Harriet Tubman's journey was a story of freedom. Knowing where she came from helped her know where she was and where she had to go.

So What Is Your Polaris?

Finding our place in the world can begin with our own personal stories. If we take time to look back on where we have been we all probably have some successes, some regrets, some hopes and fears. We freely open some doors of memory and revisit them, maybe events where we found true joy, or love and acceptance. Maybe there are other doors we prefer to remain closed—griefs, disappointments, sorrows, fears, shame. All of these make up not only who we have been, but who we are, and color and frame our view of the world. Then there's the desire to set our life story in the context of our families. One of my family memories is of my grandfather sitting at our dining room table in our home in Western New York, a suburb outside of Buffalo called West Seneca, hearing a story of who I was. "My father was a peasant in Poland," my grandfather began. "He and my mother came to this country with almost nothing, a few dollars in their pocket. They spoke almost no English, maybe enough to get by. They moved to the Polish neighborhood in Buffalo and worked hard so that I could go to school and have a better life." Then he said to me, "Your father had more education than I had and has had more opportunities than I had. And you will have more education than he did and you will have more success and opportunities." He was right. My vision of the world has become broader than that of my parents. I have had more opportunities and a lot more education. I moved away not only from my hometown, but across the country. It's the classic American Dream story many of us share, the hope for tomorrow emerging from where we have been yesterday and where we are today.

Many of us want to understand our origins more clearly. Think of the success of companies like Ancestry.com. There is a real allure of knowing exactly where we have come from. Finding our roots orients us to our place in the world and gives us a sense of identity. When my best friend, Dan, sent off a swab with his saliva to a genetic testing company, he was surprised that his family lore differed from his DNA results. He always thought he was half German, but found out he wasn't German at all. Instead, some of his ancestors were Eastern European Jews. His understanding of his ancestral journey required a course correction.

Telling the story of our ancestry has a profound hold on us. Think of people who have been adopted. Almost always they have a desire, even a longing, to know who they "really" are. Sociologist Eviatar Zerubavel talks about this in his book *Ancestors and Relatives*.[2] He quotes an adopted person saying, "I don't feel I know who I am. . . . I still feel I have no identity. I

---

2. Zerubavel, *Ancestors and Relatives*, 7.

don't think anybody can appreciate it when they have not experienced this vacuum." To know our ancestry orients us to our place in the world. "You only know where you are by memorizing where you come from."

I am not someone who easily senses where I am when I travel. I come out of a subway station in New York and have no clue what direction will lead me to my destination until I get my bearings. I am directionally challenged. Not knowing where we are can be as disorienting as not knowing who our family is. But there are even greater and more profound ways we can be disoriented.

Beyond the way we orient ourselves in place and history we also need to understand our place in the bigger picture of the cosmos. This book is about plotting our course in that much larger context so that our lives can become oriented and so we can find our Polaris. Where did we come from? Why is there something rather than nothing? Is there a bigger purpose for my life? Is there something or someone who brought this all into being?

It seems to me that even some of the longings to know our ancestry are based in these more profound longings to understand the big picture, to set ourselves in the context of something far greater than ourselves alone. We wonder whether our day-to-day ordinary lives have a greater significance. Is the map of our world simply an attempt to live the best life possible? Is there more to it?

Singer Peggy Lee gave voice to this desire in the 1960s when she sang about losing her home in a fire. As the house goes up in flames she wonders if that's all there is. Then she remembers going to the circus and being so excited, but then after it's over wondering if that's all there is. Then she thinks back on losing the love of her life and wondering again if that's all there is. Finally, she tells us that when she faces death, "that final disappointment," she'll still ask if that's all there is. The message is that there isn't anything beyond our present life, so we should just keep dancing, "break out the booze and have a ball."[3]

Our homes and our possessions often anchor us in the world; they give us a sense of place. Our experiences help form us and give us perspective.

---

3. "Is That All There Is?" written by Jerry Leiber and Mike Stoller.

Our loves and relationships help us know who we are, and yet all these are ephemeral. Even those we love most deeply will be gone someday—and so will we. Is that all there is? It seems that a lot of people agree with Peggy Lee. They tell a great cosmic story to help ground themselves in a world in which there is nothing more than the day-to-day life we live until we take our last breath. Any story that helps us understand the cosmos and our place in it will give a certain logic to our lives. It's called a cosmology: the logic of the cosmos.

A Secular Age

If you and I lived five hundred years ago and looked with wonder at the starry sky, as I did on that night on a boat in the middle of the St. Lawrence River, we would in all likelihood know the answer to the great cosmic questions. We would not even question the existence of God. It would have been our taken-for-granted assumption about the world. But about the time of the Renaissance and certainly with the dawning of the modern world in the seventeenth and eighteenth centuries, a shift began to take place. The assumptions of our Western culture began to be questioned, at first by philosophers and scientists, but in time by many ordinary people who came to believe that we are alone in the universe.

A study of more than thirty-five thousand Americans by the Pew Research Center demonstrates a shift in religious belonging. While the majority of Americans (about seven in ten) still claim to be part of the Christian faith, that number has been declining. In seven years (from 2007 to 2014) the number of self-professed Christians dropped almost 8 percent. At the same time, those describing themselves as atheist, agnostic, or "nothing in particular" increased from 16 percent to nearly 23 percent.[4]

Believing there is no God and that all there is has come about through chance wasn't first conceived in the modern era. Stephen Greenblatt tells the story of how the ancient Roman poet and philosopher Lucretius writing two thousand years ago anticipated the swerve the modern world has

---

4. Pew Research Center, May 12, 2015.

taken. He believed the whole universe was composed of atoms constantly forming and reforming. Reflecting on this ancient philosopher's vision of the world, Greenblatt tells us:

> When you look up at the night sky, and feeling unaccountably moved, marvel at the numberless stars, you are not seeing the handiwork of the gods or a crystalline sphere detached from our transient world. You are seeing the same material world of which you are a part and from whose elements you are made. There is no master plan, no divine architect, no intelligent design. All things, including the species to which you belong, have evolved over vast stretches of time. . . . But nothing—from our own species to the planet on which we live to the sun that lights our days—lasts forever. Only atoms are immortal.[5]

The seeds of Lucretius's map of the world and his view of reality have borne fruit in the world in which we live. Contemporary Western culture takes for granted a disenchanted world, one in which mystery doesn't go beyond the farthest reaches of space, or the invisible world of the smallest subatomic particle. This is a material world and it can be mapped, probed, investigated. It can come under our control. And we can in principle master all things by calculation, as the great sociologist Max Weber once wrote. Our world is one in which science measures all reality and if we can't measure it, it doesn't exist.

In the past two centuries—really in the past fifty to one hundred years—astonishing advancements in science and technology have taken place that people five hundred years ago could never have dreamed. But all of these advances, as wonderful as they are, really chart the course of the world we can know through investigation. We can explore the origins of life billions of years ago at the "Big Bang"; we can postulate the possibility of multiverses through quantum physics. We can learn more and more about our own DNA, map the depths of the human brain, find cures for diseases of all kinds, and yet the question of the significance of

---

5. Greenblatt, *The Swerve*, 5–6.

our lives—whether there is more than the eternal structuring of atoms in infinite reconfigurations—remains beyond the scope of our scientific and technological ways of knowing.

In a world view that denies the possibility of a grander scheme, the vastness of the cosmos becomes in one sense very small. The view of the world taken for granted by a great many people is a secular one; that is, a world where there is no need for a creator or anything beyond the scientifically verifiable. "A secular age," writes philosopher Charles Taylor, "is one in which the eclipse of all goals beyond human flourishing becomes conceivable, or better, it falls within the range of imaginable life for masses of people."[6]

This secular story is one map of the universe available to us. In this view, what guides us? What is our Polaris? In our one-dimensional world, the great goal for our own lives, for humankind, and for the planet is to flourish, to live the best life we can here and now. The definition of the good life is determined by what seems best to bring a sense of happiness. While scientists tell us there are defined laws governing nature and the universe, there is no sense of any kind of divine or universal law to govern our actions. Rather, we contract with one another in society to determine what is best for us—what Charles Taylor calls self-sufficing humanism. In this story we chart our own course both as individuals and communities. We seek our own understanding of happiness.

Yet, despite our desires and aspirations, we all will die and we will never fully achieve the happiness we hope for. This was the problem the great modern philosopher Albert Camus struggled with. On the one hand, we seek meaning and happiness, something beyond ourselves, but on the other, the universe is ultimately silent. In his poem "Do Not Go Gentle into That Good Night," Dylan Thomas gave voice to the absurdity and the frustration of a world where, despite our desire for eternity, we are met with finitude. Rather than accept our ultimate end, we must "rage, rage against the dying of the light."[7]

---

6. Taylor, *A Secular Age*, 19.
7. Thomas, *Collected Poems*, 193.

When the map of our world looks like this, every individual is encouraged to heroically create something for themselves. Indeed, this is the self-made person described in the anthem of the modern world made famous by Frank Sinatra, that when we face the "final curtain" we should be proud that we never knelt before any power greater than ourselves. We can proclaim, "I did it my way."[8]

But was it really? To assert that we are rugged individuals who have in a sense created ourselves belies a greater truth, that we are the products of the whole movement of the cosmos, albeit an infinitesimally small part. This truth leads to another way of understanding ourselves in the universe, whether we believe in a creator or not. We are not really individuals who can create ourselves by our own will. We are in fact linked to other human beings, to other creatures and the planet. We depend on all other life for our own. Still the illusion of self-sufficiency frames many people's view of the world. How many times has "My Way" been requested at funerals and memorials as the epitaph for the lives of so many people in our culture? I imagine Peggy Lee and Frank Sinatra drinking a final martini before last call.

The maps of reality emerging in the secular age share a common logic as to our place in the cosmos. We live out our days in the face of a final curtain and when the lights go out that's all there is. The atoms and molecules that made up our physical body will once again be recycled into the great swarm of universal dust that once found its way from ancient stars and for the briefest of moments made us conscious of the universe.

Could There Be More?

But is there another answer? If you are reading this book, you probably think that such an answer is at least possible and you are seeking to explore what is the overarching meaning of your life and the cosmos. Actually, the work of contemporary scientists may help us glimpse into that possibility. In their book *The Grand Design*, Stephen Hawking and Leonard Mlodinow

---

8. "My Way," lyrics by Paul Anka, music by Claude François.

note that it is possible to explore the universe—indeed the multiple possible universes that may exist—without invoking the existence of a creator. Even though they don't hold out the possibility of a creator, if we follow the logic of their argument, to suggest there is a first cause or creator, a designer of the grand design, is also a possibility. We can't know one way or another using the tools of verification available to us through the scientific method.

Hawking and Mlodinow believe that we can come to understand the cosmos through what they call "model dependent realism." If we look at the world through the lens of a goldfish in a bowl, our perception of reality is very different than if we look at the world from another point of view. Our perception helps create our reality. We create models or maps to interpret the world around us based on what we think is possible. "Our perception—and hence the observations on which our theories are based—is not direct, but rather is shaped by a kind of lens, the interpretive structure of our human brains."[9] In other words, everything we know about the world is defined by the limits of our map of reality. For a goldfish in a bowl, reality is bounded by the water and the space to swim. But what if one day the goldfish could swim in the ocean?

The idea of a model that frames our whole view of the world is a useful construct when we talk about belief in a creator. It is in a sense a new layer we overlay on our map of the universe. In this way, we don't contradict or evaluate the model of the cosmos created by scientific theory or experimentation. It is one dimension of reality. Rather, the belief in a creator gives us a greater depth of understanding of the cosmos and our place in it, a broader dimension of reality, a move from the goldfish bowl to a whole new and expansive sea of what exists far beyond what we can measure.

Despite our modern skepticism, there is still a hunger for believing and knowing a creator. The *New York Times* interviewed contemporary artist David Hockney. While he doesn't affiliate with any particular faith, he claims that, although he still believes he may be headed for oblivion, he believes in a personal God. "OK, you've got the big bang, but what's before

9. Hawking and Mlodinow, *Grand Design*, ch. 7, "The Apparent Miracle."

the big bang? I mean, you're always going to ask, aren't you?"[10] What came before anything else existed is a question for scientific people in the modern world much as it has been for people since the beginning of time.

We take a leap of faith whether we say there is a creator or there is not. And once we say there is a creator, we have said little about who that creator is—only that one exists. There are many ways human beings have come to understand their beliefs about a divine source of all things. Our understanding, however, is always limited by our map of the cosmos, the lens of our experience, culture, history.[11] This book will provide such a map based on the ancient stories of the Jewish and Christian traditions. It will explore one particular way of coming to know the creator. It is a story of belief in a personal God who has sought to meet us as we are. As we tell this story we will come to know more deeply a way to navigate the world around us, to find our way in the darkness. And yet, this story, as much as I believe in it, is only a glimpse of the story of that cosmic creator who will always elude our grasp and all our attempts to define, map, and measure.

Finding Our Way in the Dark

On the night before Easter many Christians around the world gather for an ancient ritual that has taken place for nearly two thousand years called the Great Vigil. The service begins in darkness. A few years ago, in my particular congregation, St. John's Cathedral in Los Angeles, we decided we would begin in total darkness. We turned out all the lights. What we hadn't thought through was that it is hard to find your way in the dark. As the participants entered the great nave of the cathedral, we carefully crept along touching pillars and almost stumbling as we helped one another to find our places.

---

10. Nayeri, "*A Bright Window*."

11. The purpose of this book is not to extend an argument about belief, unbelief, or the existence of a creator. It is my assumption that the reader of this book already has initially made that decision. However, if you would like to explore this issue further I suggest looking at *Why Believe*, by the philosopher John Cottingham (Cottingham 2009).

While we learned we should have been in our seats before we turned out the lights, I learned something ritually important about beginning in darkness: that's where we all begin. We stumble along trying to find our way, helping each other. We need to find our bearings—like Harriet Tubman on her way from slavery to freedom; like Andrew, navigating the St. Lawrence River; like the crew of the Hōkūle'a. We look up into the night sky and see the stars and wonder if we have a place and what our place is. There is a place for you. There is a creator who has a grand design for the cosmos and for your life.

Bright Morning Star arising,
Bright Morning Star arising,
Bright Morning Star arising,
Day is a-breaking in my soul![12]

Questions for Reflection

1. Nainoa Thompson, who planned the trip of the Hawaiian canoe *Hōkūle'a*, says, "You only know where you are by memorizing where you come from." Where do you come from? What in your family story or background has shaped you into who you are today?

2. We live in an age where belief in God is no longer taken for granted. How does a belief in God, or not, shape how you understand the world?

3. Science provides us a way of knowing based on assumptions of verifiability. Have you experienced other ways of knowing that can't be proved or verified? How is faith a way of knowing?

---

12. Words of a traditional Appalachian hymn. Some versions use the plural "morning stars," but the original probably is singular and refers to Jesus as the bright Morning Star used in the New Testament; see 2 Pet. 1:19 and Rev. 22:16.

2

Creating

Tell the story for our modern times.
Find the beginning.

—Homer, *The Odyssey*

In the beginning, the night sky, Tucomish, sat brooding and silent with the earth mother, Tanowish. Tucomish said, "I am older than you." Tanowish said, "I am stronger than you." So they argued between themselves. The night caused the earth to fall into a deep sleep. When she woke up she knew something had happened and that she was going to give birth. She asked the night, "What have you done?" "Nothing, you were asleep," he said. Soon within her grew all things. She sat erect and round and brought forth Wyot, her first born. He was to take care of all her other children. Soon grasses, trees, birds—everything that exists came forth from Tanowish, the great earth mother.[1]

---

1. DuBois, "Mythology of the Mission Indians."

This is a creation story of the Luiseño people native to Southern California, the land where I live. It is a cosmology not unlike the ancient creation myths of people around the world and even the cosmology of modern science. Myths invest the cosmos with meaning. They orient us to who we are and our place in the world. Scientific cosmologies attempt to look at data and provide plausible theories as to the origin of the universe, or the existence of multiple universes. From our scientific mindset, we might discount ancient cosmologies as the quaint stories of primitive peoples. We know better, we might say. Yet the two types of cosmology are different in their purposes. A scientific explanation of the cosmos may expound the nature of the universe, but naturalistic explanations aren't the only explanation of our place in the cosmos. Truth goes beyond simply describing the "facts" of how we got here.

Mythic stories can also be profoundly true because they give us insight into who we are, where we come from, and where we are going. The Luiseño creation story helps us understand that all created things are related to us. They are our brothers and sisters. This is the way this ancient people understood their place in the world. The same can be said for the stories that shaped the world of the Bible.

If we know anything of the Bible, we probably are aware of the creation story; actually two creation stories appear in the beginning of the book of Genesis, a title that itself means the book of origins. We begin our discussion with another cosmology that existed in the ancient world and how the stories in Genesis radically differ from this account. Stay with me as we go on a little historical side trip.

By the Rivers of Babylon

There were many creation stories in the ancient Near East. One in particular is from Babylon, called the Enuma Elish, and it dates back to the Bronze Age. Mesopotamian culture developed one of the first forms of writing. Perhaps these stories are older than the oral traditions. This ancient story says that in the beginning the gods were mingled as one and earth and heaven had no names. Apsu, the god of fresh water, and Tiamat, the goddess of the oceans, gave birth to many gods. Their children became so noisy that Apsu suggested to Tiamat that they destroy all their children so he could get some sleep. Tiamat was furious, but Apsu wanted to go ahead with his plan. Their child Ea, god of rivers, heard about the plot and killed his father. He built a great palace on his father's waters and became the father of a great giant, Marduk, god of storms.

When Tiamat found out Ea had killed his father, she set out to destroy him, but Marduk came to his defense. After a tense battle, Marduk killed Tiamat and split her body in two. One half he placed in the sky and made the heavens, the stars, and the moon. From the other half he made the earth and all things growing and living on it. He enslaved the vanquished gods who had fought against him on Tiamat's side. He made them work on the earth, but they soon became tired of working the fields and they rebelled. Among them was Tiamat's great champion and husband, the god Kingu. Ea and Marduk slew Kingu and they mixed his blood with clay and spittle from the other gods to create humankind and free the gods from their labors. The humans were set to toil in the fields, to raise crops and livestock, to worship, to serve the gods, and to offer sacrifice.

If origin stories orient us to our place within the world, this creation story has some powerful implications for how the people who told it understood themselves and their culture. According to this story, human beings are the slaves of the gods and serve them through the ritual worship of offering sacrifices and the sweat of human labor. The story has another implication: if power comes through violence and the gods found others to do their work, then maybe that is the divine order for human society as well. The powerful will overcome the weak in imitation of the gods and the weaker will serve the stronger as all human beings serve the gods.

Why should we care about a Babylonian creation story? Because it has a particular role to play in the Bible's story of creation. Around 587 BCE, the city of ancient Jerusalem was utterly destroyed. Archeological digs beneath the present-day city reveal a ferocious battle where homes were burned with their inhabitants still in them. It was an event of apocalyptic proportions for the people of Israel. The monarchy that had ruled Jerusalem and the kingdom of Judah for hundreds of years came to an end, its last king imprisoned in Babylon. The temple of Jerusalem where the worship of Israel's God had taken place was desecrated, pillaged, and destroyed. Though both the people of Israel and their faith in their God could have ended in the flames, they survived. The God of their ancestors went with them to exile in Babylon.[2]

This cataclysmic set of events shaped the story of the texts we read still today in the Hebrew Bible. Their captors took the cream of Israelite society off to Babylon. Estimates are that about twenty-five percent of the population were relocated leaving the working peasant classes behind. The writer of one of the great psalms of lamentation (Psalm 137) cries out:

> By the rivers of Babylon—there we sat down and there we wept
> when we remembered Zion.
> On the willows there we hung up our harps.
> For there our captors asked us for songs, and our tormentors asked
> for mirth, saying, "Sing us one of the songs of Zion!"
> How could we sing the Lord's song in a foreign land?
> If I forget you, O Jerusalem, let my right hand wither!
> Let my tongue cling to the roof of my mouth, if I do not remember
> you, if I do not set Jerusalem above my highest joy.
> Remember, O Lord, against the Edomites the day of Jerusalem's
> fall, how they said, "Tear it down! Tear it down! Down to its
> foundations!"
> O daughter Babylon, you devastator! Happy shall they be who pay
> you back what you have done to us!
> Happy shall they be who take your little ones and dash them
> against the rock!

In the midst of losing everything and deported to a faraway country, the citizens of Jerusalem had to remake themselves. They had to tell their story in a new land. They had to reorient themselves to a new map. Part of the story they told was the story of their origins, including the origins of the whole cosmos. They wanted to distinguish their stories from the stories the Babylonians told. In this light, the biblical creation stories are subversive; they tell a tale of freedom in the midst of slavery, of dignity in the face of humiliation. During the exile, and then in the period of

---

2. Silberman and Finkelstein, *The Bible Unearthed*, 295.

rebuilding after 539 BCE when they were allowed to return to their home-land, the early books of the Bible were finally stitched together in roughly the form we have them today. I use the word stitched because they form a sort of patchwork quilt that tells a great story stretching back in time to the beginning of all things. It is a family story that tells a mythic history of who they had been, so they could understand who they were and where they were going. This is why we have not one, but two stories of creation in the first chapters of Genesis, like two squares on a quilt stitched together.

In the Beginning: The First Story of Creation

When God began to create heaven and earth, and the earth then was welter and waste and darkness over the deep and God's breath hovering over the waters, God said, "Let there be light." And there was light. And God saw the light and it was good, and God divided the light from the darkness. And God called the light Day and the darkness He called Night. And it was evening and it was morning, first day.[3]

The writer continues to describe six days of creation. On each day the story builds as land appears, and the stars, the moon, and the sun to illumine the night and the day, plants, animals, and birds all come into being through a divine word. Finally, on the sixth day, God says:

Let us make a human in our image, by our likeness, to hold sway over the fish of the sea and the fowl of the heavens and the cattle and the wild beasts and all the crawling things that crawl upon the earth.

And God created the human in his image,
In the image of God He created him,
Male and female He created them.

And God blessed them, and God said to them, "Be fruitful and multiply and fill the earth and conquer it, and hold sway over

---

3. Gen. 1:1–5, Robert Alter translation.

the fish of the sea and the fowls of the heavens and every beast that crawls upon the earth.". . . And God saw all that God had done, and look, it was very good. And it was evening and it was morning the sixth day.[4]

What is the map of the world drawn in this cosmology? First, there is only one God and this God is able to create all things out of nothing. Second, the world isn't created out of violence, but through speaking a creative word. Third, human beings are not slaves of the gods or of other people. All humankind, male and female, are created in the image of the creator. Rather than serving this god as slaves, they are more like sons and daughters, sharing in divinity.

In this sense, human beings are God's representatives. Other ancient texts from Mesopotamia or Egypt also used the language of being made in the image of the gods, but it didn't apply to ordinary folks. Kings were created in the gods' image as a way of validating their authority to rule over their subjects as divine regents. What's amazing about the Genesis story is that it applies to everyone. All of us have the role of being regents of God, taking care of the earth on behalf of our divine parent. The ancient Jews defined themselves in opposition to their Babylonian masters, not as slaves but as sons and daughters, royal children of the divine king, created in God's image with the dignity of their humanity in the face of their subjugation.

These stories have continued to speak to oppressed peoples through time. African American spirituals, for example, call on these ancient traditions and recall that the God who brought Israel out of Egypt and Babylon would set them free as well. Ironically, the religion of slaveholders held within it the seeds of liberation and the stories of fundamental human dignity. These stories helped fuel the civil rights movement as well. Great leaders such as Dr. Martin Luther King Jr. used these rich biblical images to inspire African Americans, and all people, in the face of social oppression.

I remember a young woman at a retreat I led some years ago. She shared a story that as a teenager, every time she would go out with her

---

4. Gen. 1:26–28, 31, Robert Alter translation.

friends, her mother would always call out as she was leaving, "Remember who you are." Of course, at the time, she knew what her mom meant: don't get into trouble. Don't do anything stupid you might be ashamed of. She said that as she had gotten older, she realized there was something more profound in that message. Her mother was reinforcing her dignity as being created in the image of God and as such, she needed to treat herself and others with that same respect. The biblical stories provided for the ancient Jewish people, to other oppressed people, and even to people in our own day, a way to remember who we are. We are created in God's own image; we are beloved children.

As we look at this story of our origins, let's also look at the mission God gives humans to have dominion over the creation and then, a bit later, the mandate to "conquer" or subdue the earth. This sort of language has been used in later Christian tradition, especially in more contemporary times, as license to use up the earth's resources, but that doesn't seem to be the way it's used here. Rather, if humanity is invited to rule over the earth, we do so with the care God used in creating it. If we read the text this way, subduing the earth is more like harnessing its power and making use of its vast potential to continue the work of creation for the good of humankind. The story also lets us know that we are in an interdependent relationship with all other life. We are invited to use earth's resources, not use them up. These themes come out even more strongly in the second creation story in Genesis.

Before we continue with that story, there is one more element of this one we should explore. The first creation story ends, "And on the seventh day God finished the work that he had done, and he rested on the seventh day from all the work he had done. So God blessed the seventh day and hallowed it, because on it God rested from all the work that he had done in creation."[5] This detail of course suggests the origin of the Sabbath rest, but I also think this has implications for the way the early Jewish community understood themselves, and offers an important word for those of us who read this text today. To engage in creative work is what it means to be human, but work isn't slavery. Times of refreshment, rest, and

---

5. Gen. 2:1b–3.

contemplation also are what it means to be human. We will discuss the idea of Sabbath as a spiritual practice later in this book, but for now, think about the wisdom of this ancient advice to stop, rest, and savor our lives in a culture that seems to value us simply by what we do and how much of it we do. In Sabbath rest we reflect our divine source to contemplate, to engage in leisure and in so doing make a statement that we are more than what we do. We have inherent dignity by our very nature, created in the image and likeness of God.

A Garden in Eden: The Second Creation Story

Even if they aren't familiar with many Bible stories, most people know of Adam and Eve. They are the focus of the second creation story in the book of Genesis. This story is the work of another author and tells the story in a somewhat different way than the first. What's wonderful about the community that stitched these stories together is that they wanted to tell both stories because they both are true. They each give us wisdom about the cosmos and our place in it from a different perspective. Here is the tale the second storyteller spins:

> The Lord God fashioned the human, humus from the soil, and blew into his nostrils the breath of life, and the human became a living creature. And the Lord God planted a garden in Eden, to the east, and he placed there the human he had fashioned it. . . . And the Lord God said, 'It is not good for the human to be alone, I shall make him a sustainer beside him. And the Lord God fashioned from the soil each beast of the field and each fowl of the heavens and brought each to the human to see what he would call it, and whatever the human called the living creature, that was its name. And the human called names to all the cattle, and to the fowl of the heavens and to all the beasts of the field, but for the human no sustainer beside him was found. And the Lord God cast a deep slumber on the human, and he slept, and he took one of his ribs and closed over the flesh where it had been, and the Lord God built the rib he had taken from the human into a woman and he brought her to the human and the human said:

'This one at last, bone of my bones
And flesh of my flesh,
This one shall be called woman,
For from man was this one taken.'

. . . And the two of them were naked, the human and his
woman, and they were not ashamed."[6]

What answers to our questions about life does this story convey? What can we know about where we came from and our place in the world from this storyteller? What jumps out is the intimate relationship between the human and the creator. Here, even more than in the first story, the creator is the one who gives life; we could even say the creator "births" the human. The divine breath, spirit, gives the human life and creates both man and woman. The Hebrew word for the human is *adamah*, the one who comes from the humus, the fertile land. So Adam is not really the human's first name, but simply a description of the creature fashioned by the hand of God. The woman actually gets a name, Eve, but that doesn't happen until later in the story. We will get to that in the next chapter.

The wind, breath, and spirit that begin the first story of Genesis— "God's breath hovering over the waters"—once again appears here. Think of breathing in and out. Think of how you and I share that with each other. We are all sustained by breath. Think of your pets. Think of all living things. Even creatures of the sea are sustained by oxygen, as we are. The profound wisdom of Genesis is that we all share the same life force, sustained by the breath of the creator. That's amazing, when I think about it. I don't often though. I don't often take the time to realize that everyone I come in contact with is sustained by the same air that sustains me. Our ancient storyteller wants us to know we are all connected, not just by breath, but by being part of the same family.

Like the first story, the second one also gives us a sense that we as human beings have mastery over the other creatures of the earth. There is a wonderful playfulness between God, the humans, and the creatures in this tale. The creatures are named by the human as if to say the human

---

6. Gen. 2:7–8, 18–23, 25, Robert Alter translation.

knows them enough to name them. There is a sense here, as in the first story, that humankind "husbands" all the other creatures in the older sense of that word, as one who is a steward over a resource, one who carefully uses and manages something. We have retained this sense of the word when we refer to "animal husbandry." The writers of Genesis, as well as the wisdom of the ancient stories of Native American people, show us how we are connected to all other life. More broadly, if we see ourselves as God's regents of this world, then we need to realize our vocation as "husbanding" the earth as well. The second storyteller says God placed the human in the garden "to till it and keep it" (2:15).

So where was this garden? Did it ever exist? Yes! It exists in our hopes. It exists in God's dream for the world. Eden is that place of equilibrium, of peace, of *shalom*—the wellbeing of all things. It is the place where all is right with the world. Eden is the potential for the planet, but, as we will learn in the next chapter, we have moved outside Eden. We can dream of it, but we will never return to it—at least not on our own. Still, the dream of Eden may help us safeguard our planet. We live in a world where we can no longer neglect this ancient wisdom, or we do so at our peril.

While the creation stories imply God has "finished" creation, that's not the whole story. We know that creation continues to renew itself and move forward. We know that from the Big Bang the universe is ever expanding, changing, evolving. If we see ourselves as God's partners in the creative process—created in God's image and likeness—we play a role in the ongoing drama of creating as well, not only in the arts and culture, but in our scientific understanding of the world, in harnessing the resources of the earth, and in developing technological and medical advances meant to be shared with one another for the betterment of humankind and the planet.

We can also see each day as a new creation, the possibility of Eden. Eleanor Farjeon, a beloved English writer of children's stories and songs, is probably most famous for this text:

> Morning has broken,
> Like the first morning,
> Blackbird has spoken

Like the first bird;
Praise for the singing,
Praise for the morning,
Praise for them springing
Fresh from the Word. . .
Mine is the sunlight,
Mine is the morning,
Born of the one light
Eden saw play;
Praise with elation,
Praise every morning,
God's re-creation
Of the new day.

The simple words of this hymn reflect the great poetry of Genesis, placing us in a world fashioned by the grand design of a creator who daily is present with the potential for a new Eden and for our place as the co-creators and stewards of the planet given into our care.

The Spacious Firmament on High

I sit in the warm night of the California desert visiting my brother and sister-in-law's home in La Quinta. I look out over the rocky hills at the moonlit night and the starry sky. Coyotes sing together in the background and I wonder what it must have been like for the native people who sat in this place under this same sky a thousand years ago.

I think again of the modern cosmologists who search and probe the night sky for answers. They tell a tale using the remarkable tools of science and realize that we exist in an amazingly fine-tuned universe in which the slightest modification would result in our not existing at all. They surmise that there must be multiple universes that exist and the iteration of these universes eventually resulted in one that supports life and consciousness as we know it. Yet, as I said in the last chapter, while these theoretical constructs may in fact be real, they are difficult to verify from our vantage point of the fishbowl of our perspective. Nevertheless, to assert the world was created as an eventual probability of possible outcomes is an act of faith based on over-relying on one particular tool of knowledge to answer every question; a hammer is great to pound in a nail, but I need a tweezers to remove a sliver from my finger. Scientism—the overreliance on scientific explanations—cannot provide adequate answers to all our questions. Science and reason can take us only so far. They will accompany us to the limits of their ability, but can take us no further.

There is underlying spiritual truth, I believe, beyond the limits of what we can measure or calculate, a reality accessed through the poetic and through the human experience of God. This experience is given voice through the grand narratives of our ancient cosmologies—in particular through the wisdom of those ancient Jewish storytellers whose words retain so much power thousands of years after they were set down in writing. They are words that gave voice to stories likely far older; words that give voice to a longing and belief deep within me, longing for a connection with something, someone far greater and more immense than I am, or of which I can ever conceive.

In a very real way I think we do remember Eden. I'm struck by the words of a poem by Anne Porter.

When I was a child
I once sat sobbing on the floor
Beside my mother's piano
As she played and sang
For there was in her singing
A shy yet solemn glory
My smallness could not hold
And when I was asked
Why I was crying
I had no words for it
I only shook my head
And went on crying
Why is it that music
At its most beautiful
Opens a wound in us

An ache a desolation
Deep as a homesickness
For some far-off
And half-forgotten country
I've never understood
Why this is so
But there's an ancient legend
From the other side of the world
That gives away the secret
Of this mysterious sorrow
For centuries on centuries
We have been wandering
But we were made for Paradise
As deer for the forest
And when music comes to us
With its heavenly beauty
It brings us desolation
For when we hear it
We half remember
That lost native country
We dimly remember the fields
Their fragrant windswept clover
The birdsongs in the orchards
The wild white violets in the moss
By the transparent streams
And shining at the heart of it
Is the longed-for beauty
Of the One who waits for us
Who will always wait for us
In those radiant meadows
Yet also came to live with us
And wanders where we wander.[7]

7. "Music," by Anne Porter, from *Living Things: Collected Poems*, Steerforth Press, 2006. Reprinted with Permission from Steerforth Press.

Music and art all share in the creative spirit breathed into us. The beauty of the mountains glimpsed in the Yosemite Valley, or wherever you have experienced such grandeur, all reflect a divine hand we can touch through our spirits, to remember a far-off echo, as C. S. Lewis describes it.

The books or the music in which we thought the beauty was located will betray us if we trust to them; it was not in them, it only came through them, and what came through them was longing. These things—the beauty, the memory of our own past—are good images of what we really desire; but if they are mistaken for the thing itself they turn into dumb idols, breaking the hearts of their worshippers. For they are not the thing itself; they are only the scent of a flower we have not found, the echo of a tune we have not heard, news from a country we have never yet visited.[8]

As I look up at the sky, the poetic words of Joseph Addison and the soaring strains of Franz Joseph Haydn's magnificent reflection on creation, itself a work of tremendous beauty, echo in my mind:

The spacious firmament on high,
With all the blue ethereal sky,
And spangled heavens, a shining frame
Their great Original proclaim.
Th'unwearied sun, from day to day,
Does his creator's powers display,
And publishes to every land
The work of an almighty hand.

Soon as the evening shades prevail
The moon takes up the wondrous tale,
And nightly to the listening earth
Repeats the story of her birth;
While all the stars that round her burn
And all the planets in their turn,
Confirm the tidings as they roll,
And spread the truth from pole to pole.

---

8. Lewis, *The Weight of Glory*, 30–31.

What though in solemn silence all
Move round the dark terrestrial ball?
What though no real voice nor sound
Amid the radiant orbs be found?
In reason's ear they all rejoice,
And utter forth a glorious voice,
Forever singing as they shine,
The hand that made us is divine.[9]

Yet, this is not the end of the story. The epic tale of the Bible begins in Eden, but it also reflects on the more complex narrative of human life. We are people who have lost our bearings and the biblical story tells a great tale of being lost and being found.

A fire is set on a dark night in the middle of the dark nave of a cathedral in early spring. Slowly the columns of a great Romanesque building are illumined by the flames; the faces of those gathered on this night soon glow in the light. This is the night before the Great Feast of Easter, and as Christians gather, we begin by lighting this fire and tell our story by its light. This is the story of the Bible.

Questions for Reflection

1. C. S. Lewis says we hear an "echo of a tune we have not heard, news from a country we have never yet visited." Have you experienced that longing for spiritual connection Lewis discovered? In what ways? Can you tell a story about these connections in your own life?

2. Read Anne Porter's poem "Music" again. What images stand out for you? Have you ever experienced the longing the poem expresses?

---

9. Words by Joseph Addison, in *The Spectator*, London, August 23, 1712. Music from *Creation*, Franz J. Haydn, 1798.

3. Eden is always a possibility, but an elusive one. What do the Bible's stories of creation tell us about who we are, who God is, and how we relate to the planet, to one another, and to God?

4. What do you think of when you look out into the vastness of the night sky? How do you fit in?

3

Wandering

The morning news aired in the background as I was getting ready to leave for work on September 11, 2001. I remember being transfixed by what I saw unfolding before my eyes. Suddenly the world was changing. I was planning to leave the next day to fly to New York; I was scheduled to preach at St. Luke's Church not far from the World Trade Center. In fact, my colleague Dan who at that time was on the staff at St. Luke's witnessed the second plane crash into the tower. The horror of that day is still difficult to comprehend. The choice of a few people deluded by zealotry brought death to thousands.

This is just one extraordinary example of human violence and sin. Each day in our nation and around the world we see others, some small, some great. Some are the events that make the news; some are the personal choices we make through our words, our actions, and the things we fail to do. Real human beings choose the good or choose to do wrong with very real consequences. Certainly, the choices we make are constrained by a whole web of forces often beyond our control. Despite all we have said about the original goodness of creation and of human beings created in the image of God, there is also the capacity for tremendous evil both individually and corporately. Both things are true. Our Christian tradition has

tried to come to grips with our human nature both to describe our goodness and the evil of which we are capable. We begin with a story.

A Pear Tree

Late at night, a group of teenage boys roam around the roads of their rural
town looking for trouble. One boy's family owns a vineyard and next door
there is pear tree full of ripe fruit. The boys get some buckets and fill them
up with pears. They eat a couple of them, but mostly it's the fun of steal-
ing from the neighbor's tree and then going off to throw pears at the pigs
on the next farm. Those boys come from good families and have plenty to
eat. It's a thoughtless teenage prank. Most of them probably forgot about it
after they went to bed that night.

One boy didn't forget. Many decades later, as an old man staring out
the window from his writing desk, he recalls that night. It's a story that
sticks in his mind because it makes him think about the dark side of our
human nature. His name is Augustine and he wrote an autobiographical
meditation on his life called *Confessions*. Since that night he led a life as
a pagan philosopher, a philanderer, and after his conversion, a Christian
who became bishop of the North African city of Hippo as the Roman
Empire crumbled around him in the fourth century.

The story of the pear tree caused Augustine to think about another
tree: the tree of the knowledge of good and evil in the book of Genesis.
Augustine knew that we are created good. There is a desire within us to
create, to love, to be in relationship with one another. There is an echo of
Eden, of our union with our Creator deep in our spirits. Yet we desire to
live life on our own terms. We have a tendency towards selfishness, to love
things that are forbidden simply because we can. We seek to captain our
own ship.

Maybe you and I have seen within ourselves a tendency to wrongdoing, pride, self-will, stubbornness, or turning a blind eye to the needs of
others. We can look out at our world and see the fruit of those human
tendencies. If we look at the bigger picture of the world around us, we see

the results of wars, terrorism, greed, ecological devastation, hunger, and poverty. Unfortunately, one of the most empirically verifiable elements of Christian doctrine is the existence of evil in the world. The echo of Eden in our hearts reminds us of the possibility of a world where we are in right relationship with one another and with our Creator; when we observe how off-kilter things are, we know the world needs to be put right.

Certainly such a realization is not new to contemporary culture, or even to the world of the late Roman Empire when Augustine wrote. Many centuries before, the people who brought us the Bible also realized the human tendency toward evil. In fact, the second story of creation in the book of Genesis continues with the tale of how the man and the woman in the garden fractured their relationship with God. No longer was everything right with the world.

The Tree of the Knowledge of Good and Evil

One of the most famous stories in the Bible depicted in art and retold in various ways throughout the generations concerns Adam, Eve, a fruit tree in the Garden of Eden, and a serpent. The people who first spun this tale did not write a history of how the first human beings lost their innocence. Rather, like Augustine's reflection on the pear tree, they wrote to help us understand the complexity of the human predicament by means of a story:

> The serpent was clever, more clever than any wild animal God had made. He spoke to the Woman: "Do I understand that God told you not to eat from any tree in the garden?"
>
> The Woman said to the serpent, "Not at all. We can eat from the trees in the garden. It's only about the tree in the middle of the garden that God said, 'Don't eat from it; don't even touch it or you'll die.'"
>
> The serpent told the Woman, "You won't die. God knows that the moment you eat from that tree, you'll see what's really going on. You'll be just like God, knowing everything, ranging all the way from good to evil."

When the Woman saw that the tree looked like good eating and realized what she would get out of it—she'd know everything!—she took and ate the fruit and then gave some to her husband, and he ate.[1]

Over the centuries people have wondered what kind of fruit was the object of that first temptation. Popular culture has imagined the forbidden fruit as an apple. Maybe it was a pear, like the fruit that tempted Augustine. In earlier times, people imagined a pomegranate. It was an enticing object of desire. Remember, this story didn't happen in a specific historic place and time. The temptation of the first woman and man is an allegory, and as such we can say the story of our temptation and expulsion from Eden never happened, or, better still, it always is happening.

The fruit of that tree can be bitter indeed. Billie Holiday sang about "strange fruit" in a ballad describing the hatred of racism in the southern United States where black men were lynched without even a semblance of justice, hanging as if they were fruit. As the lyrics conclude: "Here is a strange and bitter crop."[2] Tales of lynching may no longer be the norm in our nation, yet we still experience the bitter fruit of racism, death, and violence of all sorts. Real human beings make choices. We continue to eat the strange and bitter fruit of the tree of the knowledge of good and evil and our choices bear fruit and impact the real lives of people.

The tale we read in the third chapter of Genesis is about making a choice. The woman and the man chose not to do good and, by choosing instead to do evil, they experienced for themselves the difference between the two. To eat that fruit was to make a decision: I'll do it my way. I will listen to the wisdom of the creature rather than the Creator. Even more, it demonstrated a lack of faith in the ultimate love of the Creator for the human beings with whom the Creator was in intimate relationship as a parent loving a child. There was a fundamental lack of trust. Once that decision was made, the relationship was altered. Walking away from God and making a choice to do evil rather than good is an option for all of us.

---

1. Gen. 3:1–6, CEB.
2. "Strange Fruit," written by Dwayne P. Wiggins, Maurice Pearl, and Lewis Allan.

The choice the woman and the man made was not simply to disobey, but to acquire more than they needed. They could have had fruit from all the trees of the garden, including the tree of life, but that was not enough. They wanted it all. The desire not to be denied anything is something from which we suffer acutely in our culture. We have not learned our lesson from Eden. Writing in 1997 in *The Atlantic*, noted environmental philosopher Mark Sagoff cautioned:

> The world has the wealth and the resources to provide everyone the opportunity to live a decent life. We consume too much when market relationships displace the bonds of community, compassion, culture, and place. We consume too much when consumption becomes an end in itself and makes us lose affection and reverence for the natural world.[3]

In the years since Sagoff warned us about our habits of consumption, we have become so much more aware of the great threat consumerism poses to the planet due to global warming. As Genesis teaches us, our environmental problems are primarily moral and spiritual, not simply economic or social. The creator entrusts the earth into our hands, to till it and to keep it for the benefit of humankind and with care for all life on the planet.

The Serpent

So what about the sly, slithering serpent? When I hear the serpent's subtle suggestions, and when I realize the story is an allegory, I begin to understand the serpent's words as an interior voice tempting with the promise of no limits and unending life. The serpent suggested to the woman that there was a way to have whatever she wanted and to live forever. The problem was that God was keeping that secret from her. The serpent wanted her to think God was to be feared, not loved.

---

3. Sagoff, "Do We Consume Too Much?," online edition.

We humans, created in the image of God, seek to explore wisdom: to learn, to create, to know what we do not know, to explore, to map the terrain of the world. The insidious and sly suggestions of the serpent turn that natural curiosity on its head. Remember earlier in the story, God gives humanity a vocation to use our natural gifts to help sustain and enhance the created order. We are invited to husband the creatures of the earth, to learn about them, to harness the power of nature for the good of ourselves and the world. Here that natural curiosity is turned inward, to benefit the self alone. Even stranger is the turn in the relations between the human and the serpent. Rather than have mastery over the fish of the sea and the birds of the air, as the first creation story tells us, it seems the serpent gains mastery over the human. The natural order has been subtly subverted. All is not right with the world. To riff on Shakespeare, something's rotten in the state of nature.

In the Christian tradition, evil—the force working contrary to God—has been understood to have a tremendous power, which we call Satan, or the devil. That evil energy, personified allegorically in the serpent, is not simply a shadow side within our own psyche, but is an objective reality. That dark force works within the world and destroys the beauty of the creation as God has created it, including the lives of human beings. The good news of the Christian story is that the dark force never has the last word. There is always hope beyond the darkness that often envelops the world.

Lest we think dark forces and Satan are no longer relevant to our society, we should think about the hold such images have on popular culture even in our own day. In the Harry Potter novels, for example, Voldemort, the dark lord, personifies the force of evil and death. In *Game of Thrones*, the Night King and the White Walkers have the power to reanimate the dead as a destructive force of evil. Why, in our rationalist society, do such images of powerful dark forces still capture our imagination? Maybe it's because there is a strong deep sense within us that such a dark force exists and that we have the choice to participate in it or not. And yet, as we will discuss later, such a decision to choose the good and fight on the side of light is not simply an act of our own will. Our contemporary myths also imagine the need for a champion to assist us in this great cosmic battle. We cannot win on our own.

The Christian tradition says there is a matrix of evil in the world that holds us and constrains our ability to choose the good. We call this power over us "original sin." As Christians reflect on the Genesis story of the fall of humans, we see in it a mirror of our own lives. All of us can identify with Adam and Eve if we look at ourselves honestly. The early Christian writer and apostle Paul wrote a letter to the Christian church in Rome. He gave voice to the human predicament:

> [T]he power of sin within me keeps sabotaging my best intentions, I obviously need help! I realize that I don't have what it takes. I can will it, but I can't do it. I decide to do good, but I don't really do it; I decide not to do bad, but then I do it anyway. My decisions, such as they are, don't result in actions. Something has gone wrong deep within me and gets the better of me every time.
>
> It happens so regularly that it's predictable. The moment I decide to do good, sin is there to trip me up. I truly delight in God's commands, but it's pretty obvious that not all of me joins in that delight. Parts of me covertly rebel, and just when I least expect it, they take charge.
>
> I've tried everything and nothing helps. I'm at the end of my rope. Is there no one who can do anything for me? Isn't that the real question?[4]

Paul, a Jewish teacher who had a mystical experience of Jesus, came to believe that as hard as he might try to live according to the pattern of life God intended in creation, he could never extract himself from the stranglehold of human wrongdoing. Maybe the serpent is like a boa constrictor that just won't let go. For Paul and for us, there is good news about how we can become untangled; we'll explore that way out later.

---

4. Rom. 7:17b–24, *The Message*, by Eugene Peterson, 2002. *The Message* is a compelling paraphrase Bible and presents a good telling of this story. You can compare this version with an actual translation, such as the one found in the New Revised Standard Version of the Bible.

Naked

The writer of this story in Genesis gives us this detail: "And the man and his wife were both naked, and were not ashamed" (Genesis 2:25). The man and the woman were vulnerable, uncovered before one another and before God. Yet something happens in the story, after the man and the woman eat the forbidden fruit:

> Immediately the two of them did "see what's really going on"— saw themselves naked! They sewed fig leaves together as makeshift clothes for themselves.
>
> When they heard the sound of God strolling in the garden in the evening breeze, the Man and his Wife hid in the trees of the garden, hid from God.
>
> God called to the Man: "Where are you?"
>
> He said, "I heard you in the garden and I was afraid because I was naked. And I hid."
>
> God said, "Who told you you were naked? Did you eat from that tree I told you not to eat from?"
>
> The Man said, "The Woman you gave me as a companion, she gave me fruit from the tree, and, yes, I ate it."
>
> God said to the Woman, "What is this that you've done?"
>
> "The serpent seduced me," she said, "and I ate."[5]

The man and woman put on fig leaves to cover up their shame. Have you ever felt a fig leaf? It's kind of like sand paper. Fig leaves are uncomfortable. They are like the masks we sometimes put up to hide ourselves from the world. They are like the armor we wear to make the world think we are strong and invulnerable. But what are we trying to hide? Are we ashamed?

Brené Brown has done extensive research on the problem of shame in our culture. She has interviewed thousands of men and women about their experience of shame. She says shame is first of all the fear of disconnection. "We are psychologically, emotionally, cognitively, and spiritually

---

5. Gen. 3:7–12, msg.

hard-wired for connection, love and belonging." Here's how she defines shame: "The intensely painful feeling or experience of believing that we are flawed and therefore unworthy of love and belonging."[6]

The woman and the man in the garden were shamed. They hid themselves. They covered up with fig leaves. They no longer believed they could be naked, vulnerable to God or one another. They not only believed they had done something bad, they believed they were bad. Shame is a question of identity. Shame says we are not worthy of love and connection. Brenè Brown makes a helpful distinction between shame and guilt. When we have done something we know is wrong and we look at our best and truest selves—who we want to be and become—guilt may help us acknowledge the wrong and give us impetus to move beyond it and learn from our mistakes. Shame paralyzes us and enables the disconnection we most fear.

I find this to be a powerful story for my life. It's easy to confuse shame and guilt. There's a difference between who I am and what I do. Rather than using guilt as a means of self-examination, I've allowed shame to paralyze me into thinking I am a fraud and not able to be who I want to be. Big difference.

When I was a graduate student I taught a course in ethics for adult learners at a local college. One evening a woman who always sat in the front row raised her hand and asked a question about the origin of a word I had used. While I knew the concept I was trying to get across, I wasn't sure of the origin of the word and how it related to the concept. Because I didn't want to reveal the fact that I didn't know something as an insecure graduate student, I took a guess and delivered my response with great authority. Well, what I didn't know was that she had been waiting for an opportunity to find the chink in my armor and the next week she came back to class loaded for bear. She raised her hand and began to tell me how I was wrong in my answer the previous week. I was laid bare before the students in my class. I think I probably acknowledged that she was right and that I had not had the right answer about that question. I don't exactly remember what I said because the shame monster was holding me

---

6. Brown, *Daring Greatly*, 67–68.

hostage. Driving home after class, I played all the tapes about what a loser I was. I was dumb. I was incompetent. I was ashamed.

I wonder if you have experiences when the shame tapes play over in your life. The tapes that say you are not worthy. Maybe there are even tapes that say you are not worthwhile. Maybe there are shame messages that keep you from being vulnerable, from connecting to other people or connecting to God. Maybe like the man and the woman in the garden, you don't want God to see your nakedness. God is someone you fear. In response, you put on scratchy fig leaves, build up your defenses, or blame someone else, as happens in the story in the garden. The man blames the woman for giving him the fruit to eat. The woman blames the serpent. The blame game is something we all play.

In the first chapter I mentioned my friends Tom and Thomas and their summer cottage on the St. Lawrence River. The waters of the St. Lawrence are particularly treacherous since underwater shoals lie undetectable just beneath the surface. Learning the underwater map of the river is crucial if you're going to boat in those waters. My friend Thomas learned about that the hard way. When he first tried to steer a boat down the river he underestimated the need for a good map or an expert pilot. Steering with more confidence than skill, he ran aground. So what do you do when you're in the middle of a river and your boat is on a shoal? He was lucky that some longtime residents of the river saw what happened and made their way out to rescue them and get the boat back to dock. The driver was unscathed, apart from a bruised ego, not so the boat. The propeller had to be replaced. A week later when he returned the boat, Thomas feared the worst in terms of how much a new propeller was going to cost. Instead the curmudgeonly owner of the boat company told him it wouldn't cost him anything. "I've been renting boats for thirty-five years to people who come up here thinking they know how to navigate the river. I can't tell you how many times people have done exactly what you have done, but not one of them admitted it was their fault. They always say the boat was damaged when they picked it up. You didn't. You admitted what you did. For you, it's free."

Maybe the difference between thirty-five years of not admitting fault and my friend Thomas is the difference between shame and guilt. I can't say for sure, but I know deflecting and blaming are fig leaves a lot of us use to pretend we haven't done wrong. But I think it's deeper than that. We want to do whatever we can to hide our shame. We are afraid of disconnection. We want to be loved. We want to be worthy of love, but we are afraid we aren't.

Wandering

God told the serpent:
"Because you've done this, you're cursed,
　　cursed beyond all cattle and wild animals,
Cursed to slink on your belly
　　and eat dirt all your life.
I'm declaring war between you and the Woman,
　　between your offspring and hers.
He'll wound your head,
　　you'll wound his heel."
He told the Woman:
"I'll multiply your pains in childbirth;
　　you'll give birth to your babies in pain.
You'll want to please your husband,
　　but he'll lord it over you."
He told the Man:
"Because you listened to your wife
　　and ate from the tree
That I commanded you not to eat from,
　　'Don't eat from this tree,'
The very ground is cursed because of you;
　　getting food from the ground
Will be as painful as having babies is for your wife;
　　you'll be working in pain all your life long.
The ground will sprout thorns and weeds,
　　you'll get your food the hard way,
Planting and tilling and harvesting,
　　sweating in the fields from dawn to dusk,

Until you return to that ground yourself, dead and buried;
you started out as dirt, you'll end up dirt."

The Man, known as Adam, named his wife Eve because she was the mother of all the living.

God made leather clothing for Adam and his wife and dressed them.

God said, "The Man has become like one of us, capable of knowing everything, ranging from good to evil. What if he now should reach out and take fruit from the Tree-of-Life and eat, and live forever? Never—this cannot happen!"

So God expelled them from the Garden of Eden and sent them to work the ground, the same dirt out of which they'd been made. He threw them out of the garden and stationed angel-cherubim and a revolving sword of fire east of it, guarding the path to the Tree-of-Life.[7]

You might have guessed that this story was not going to end well. This part concludes with a tragic ode about life outside of Eden, as if God was pronouncing an all but inevitable sentence on humankind. It's not a punishment; it's the consequence of wandering and living in alienation and disconnection. Writing from the perspective of the Jewish tradition, Rabbi Jonathan Magonet reflects:

When a certain innocence is lost, it cannot be recaptured, except by willfully denying the new reality. It can only be rediscovered after a long journey through the new-found knowledge; and the journey of humanity, and of each individual person, is a quest to find that state of wholeness again outside the shelter of the garden.

Then he asks a provocative question:

So did they fall or were they pushed? And is the "Fall" the cataclysm that some theologies see it as—or is it a first, necessary step towards the emancipation of humanity, the first liberation from the slavery of

---

7. Gen. 3:14–24, MSG.

the womb? Because if it is only a "fall"—then the journey back to God is either enmeshed in guilt, or so dependent on some external source of salvation that human creativity, generosity and goodness are reduced to mere irrelevances or successful strategies for a return to divine favor. But if it is a liberation, however bitter or painful it may be at the moment of separation, then human beings travel bearing a full responsibility for their life and their actions, for their choices and ultimately for their death. And in terms of biblical faith, they have also the ultimate freedom—to choose or not to choose God.[8]

I find these questions compelling, but the answers ultimately unsatisfying. Magonet asks whether embracing human freedom is to understand that we have the capacity to make of this world what we will—either a wasteland or a garden, to live connected with each other and the earth as God dreams or to live in shame and separation. In this light, we choose a relationship with God out of freedom; with that I agree. However, I am much less convinced of our ultimate ability to choose the good without the assistance of a God who continues to call out to us, a parent searching for wandering children. This is where I fall back on the wisdom of the Christian tradition. We cannot live up to who we were created to be. We live outside Eden. We tend to be wanderers and so we need not a push but a pull to bring us home again.

The story of our exile from Eden acknowledges the hardship of life, the pains and the sorrows we inevitably experience and even the death we all will one day share. There is a sense that the separation from Eden and from God cannot be reversed. We cannot return to our original innocence. Yet even here, God does not forsake us. God makes for the man and woman not fig leaves, but clothes for their journey in the wider world, signs of the ongoing love of a parent for wandering children. Much of the rest of the story of Genesis, and really the whole Bible, is about God calling, "Where are you?" God and humankind chart the territory. We are finding the way home. But before we continue with that story, there follows another tale of even greater separation and death.

---

8. Magonet, *A Rabbi*, 125.

Brother Kills Brother

In 2007 archeologists made a surprising discovery beneath the city of Rome. They found the remnants of a large domed structure they think was the Lupercal, a cave where ancient Romans believed a she-wolf suckled two semi-divine boys, children of the war god Mars and a human priestess. When the boys grew up, one of them, Romulus, killed his brother, Remus, and became the founder of the city of Rome. Each year ancient Romans celebrated the Lupercalia, ritually enacting the story of their founder's infancy and celebrating a city founded on fratricide. The power of Romulus over his brother was lived out in the Roman ideal of *virtus*, from which we get our word "virtue." For the Romans, *virtus* was primarily associated with military might and victory: "might makes right." There is another story of fratricide in the founding stories of ancient Israel. It immediately follows the story of the expulsion from Eden:

> Now the man had relations with his wife Eve, and she conceived and gave birth to Cain, and she said, "I have gotten a manchild with the help of the Lord." Again, she gave birth to his brother Abel. And Abel was a keeper of flocks, but Cain was a tiller of the ground. So it came about in the course of time that Cain brought an offering to the Lord of the fruit of the ground. Abel, on his part also brought of the firstlings of his flock and of their fat portions. And the Lord had regard for Abel and for his offering; but for Cain and for his offering He had no regard. So Cain became very angry and his countenance fell. Then the Lord said to Cain, "Why are you angry? And why has your countenance fallen? If you do well, will not your countenance be lifted up? And if you do not do well, sin is crouching at the door; and its desire is for you, but you must master it." Cain told Abel his brother. And it came about when they were in the field, that Cain rose up against Abel his brother and killed him.
>
> Then the Lord said to Cain, "Where is Abel your brother?" And he said, "I do not know. Am I my brother's keeper?" He said, "What have you done? The voice of your brother's blood is crying to Me from the ground. Now you are cursed from the ground, which has opened its mouth to receive your brother's blood from your hand. When you

cultivate the ground, it will no longer yield its strength to you; you will be a vagrant and a wanderer on the earth." Cain said to the Lord, "My punishment is too great to bear! Behold, You have driven me this day from the face of the ground; and from Your face I will be hidden, and I will be a vagrant and a wanderer on the earth, and whoever finds me will kill me." So the Lord said to him, "Therefore whoever kills Cain, vengeance will be taken on him sevenfold." And the Lord appointed a sign for Cain, so that no one finding him would slay him.

Then Cain went out from the presence of the Lord, and settled in the land of Nod, east of Eden.[9]

The difference between these two stories is striking. In the first, the very founding of a people is based on one brother killing another. In the second, fratricide results in further separation and disconnection between God and people. As I see it, one of the key differences in these two perspectives is how we conceive of human relationships: are they basically tribal or universal?

The story of Romulus and Remus was the myth that gave the Romans a sense of their identity as a conquering people. They would maintain their place in the world by overpowering other tribes. By contrast, the story of Cain and Abel tells us that every human being is the sibling of the other; we are responsible to watch over one another. If that is a meaning of this story, it has deep implications for us. Who do we watch out for?

The seeds of the imperial tribal mindset still grow in the soil of America today. A belief that our "tribe" has the right to conquer others is the root of racism and terrorism. It nourishes fear of the other. Are we responsible to build up our tribe? Or are we our brother's keeper whoever and wherever they may be?

A Beast Lying in Wait

The famous Jewish philosopher Martin Buber has an unusual translation of God's words of warning to Cain: "If thou dost purpose good, bear

---

9. Gen. 4:1–16, NASB.

it aloft, but if thou dost not purpose good—sin before the door, a beast lying in wait, unto thee his desire, but prevail thou over him." The original Hebrew text of this passage is difficult to grasp. It probably is a fragment of very ancient poetry sewn into the fabric of the story. The word "sin" first appears here in the Bible. It doesn't show up in the story of the garden. Buber notes that the concept of sin in this passage is personified as a demon, described as a wild beast. The soul of the human person has within it the ability to fall prey to this beast or to withstand him. Buber comments, "If the passage may be so understood it is the truest example within the world's early epic literature of a divine being's appeal to men to decide for the 'good,' that means to set out in the direction of the divine."[10]

But Cain does not decide for the good. He turns away and murders his brother. When God curses Cain for his deed, he gives him a destiny "which is the incarnate representation of what took place within his soul."[11] Cain's act of violence drives him farther from God into the Land of Nod, which simply means the land of wandering, the place where human beings dwell on the other side of Eden.

The embodiment of sin as a beast lying in wait reminds me of Don Winslow's novel *The Power of the Dog,* which explores international drug cartels and the intersections between poverty, crime, addiction, wealth, politics, and violence. The American drug enforcement agent, Art, reflects on the life of Adán, whom Art knew years before when Adán was a teenager. He remembers Adán as a good kid who later became a powerful drug operative caught up in the web of violence. "Whatever it was lying dormant inside him . . . maybe it lies in all of us," Art would later think. "It sure as hell did in me. The power of the dog."[12]

Later in the novel, Adán is placed in a circumstance where he is asked to murder two small children as part of a battle between drug lords. Before he carries out the crime he pauses:

---

10. Buber, *Good and Evil*, 86–87.
11. Buber, *Good and Evil*, 89.
12. Winslow, *The Power of the Dog*, 26–27.

It is at this precise moment that he understands the nature of evil, that evil has a momentum of its own, which, once started is impossible to stop. It's the law of physics—a body at rest tends to stay at rest; a body set in motion tends to stay in motion." He goes on to reflect, "a man who would never have the weakness to set a great evil into motion doesn't have the strength to stop it once its moving. The hardest thing in the world isn't to refrain from committing an evil, it's to stand up and stop one.[13]

The momentum of evil is especially powerful when we collude with one another and incite each other to wrongdoing. When Augustine remembered the theft of the pears from the neighbor's tree, he recalled that he would never have done it by himself. It was only the mutual experience that both encouraged those teenage boys to act as they did and increased their thrill of doing it. "What an exceedingly unfriendly form of friendship that was!" He would write in *Confessions*:

> It was a seduction of the mind hard to understand, which instilled into me a craving to do harm for sport and fun. I was greedy for another person's loss without any desire on my part to gain anything or to settle a score. Let the others only say, "Come on, let's go and do it!" and I am ashamed to hold back from the shameless act.[14]

Augustine's reflections not only remind us of what we all might know about adolescent peer pressure, but also about how a shameful act becomes more acceptable when validated by others, or by a community. We can see this in the chilling rallies held by Adolph Hitler in Nazi Germany where thousands of people were emboldened and energized not only by the hate speech and oratory of the man himself, but by the collective effervescence of the crowd. We can see it in racism in our own nation when mob mentality bore the strange fruit hanging from the poplar trees—the power of the dog, the beast crouching at the door.

---

13. Winslow, *The Power of the Dog*, 294.
14. Augustine, *Confessions*, book 2, ch. 9.

Driving home one evening, I listened to a discussion of the documentary film *Audrie and Daisy* about two teenage girls who were from different places, but had similar experiences of being drunk and then sexually abused by teenage boys. Afterwards both were publicly shamed online by their peers. Audrie's story is particularly poignant. In 2012 she attended a back-to-school party where alcohol was plentiful; she passed out after having had too much to drink. Three of her classmates stripped her, wrote obscene messages on her body with indelible markers, and took sexually explicit photos of her. The images were published on the internet. Afterward she posted, "I now have a reputation that I can never get rid of. . . . My life is over." Within a week she had killed herself.

The young men who violated Audrie's body and her dignity and the other young people who shamed her on social media were not in themselves more evil than anyone else. They participated in a trajectory of misdeeds that took on a life bigger than themselves. They unleashed the power of the dog. Yet, there is a sense in which actions like these can more easily happen when there is no moral compass guiding us, no conscience formed within us to prevent us from deciding to do wrong.

I tell Audrie's story because it seems to me an example of a culture in which human life has been cheapened and where human beings are objectified and commodified. When we are thought simply to exist in a universe empty of any greater logic or design, if what is right is simply what we make of it, then what is the foundation for our fundamental human dignity?

The map of the cosmos in which we are children of a divine creator allows us to remember who we are and to respect the dignity of every human being. It is true that we can respect other human beings without reference to God, but on what objective basis? Without a sense of a divinely ordered universe, our beliefs about human dignity are mutable and simply a matter of social contract. Instead, I think of Audrie as I hear again the ancient words of the writer of the first chapter of Genesis call across the ages:

So God created humankind in his image,
in the image of God he created them;
Male and female he created them.

Many of us may not have engaged in extreme acts of violence, but we all know what it's like to wander, to experience shame and guilt. We all know what it's like to do things we are not proud of or to fail to do what we ought to have done. We are children of Adam and Eve. Yet God calls out to each of us, "Where are you?" Will we turn around and set out back in the direction of the divine? That in effect is what the word "repentance" means—to turn around, to correct course. But can we get there on our own? How can we know the way?

Back to the Garden?

In the summer of 1969 an event occurred that transformed American culture. A music festival dubbed *An Aquarian Exposition: 3 Days of Peace and Music* lasted four days in August. It became the formative experience of the Woodstock Generation, as they came to be called, named after the festival's location on Max Yasgur's farm near the town of Woodstock, New York. In an era rocked by the violence of the Vietnam War, racial unrest, and calls for civil rights and equality, Woodstock became the symbol of the hope that peace, love, and justice might be possibilities. The singer Joni Mitchell penned the anthem that gave voice to the optimism of this young generation. Her song "Woodstock" told an almost mythic story of the hopes and fears of the experience. Her words give voice to the youthful optimism they shared and the deep longing to return to the garden, to Eden, the place of right relationship, an end to violence, and the vision of peace among all earth's creatures.

That was the hope of the Woodstock generation: that they could set out on the path back to the garden through our own best efforts. Despite those beautiful aspirations, there was no clear knowledge of how to get there. And maybe they underestimated the tremendous power of evil in the human heart causing us to turn away from the good. Yet, I believe the call of Woodstock was a response to the echo of the voice of God calling, "Where are you?" But there was no sense of the need for God to set them on the path, to provide the North Star to guide the course. In fact, where did the Woodstock generation lead us?

There have been tremendous strides in movements toward equality for African Americans, women, gays and lesbians, but racism and the fear of the other are still ugly forces in our society. The impacts of war, terrorism, and violence have grown worse, not better. Global warming is destroying our environment. Are we much closer to the dream of Eden?

On our own, we are much like what Albert Camus says in his retelling of the Greek myth of Sisyphus: we humans continually push a boulder up a mountain only to see it roll back down again. Camus did not believe in a god. He thought human striving to achieve good would never result in ultimate change; in the end, we die. The struggle itself was enough for him. Maybe we can call that continual wandering until the lights go out. I believe there is more. The struggle is not all there is. There is a way home, but we cannot get ourselves back to the garden. We need someone to show us the way. To seek the good is not to roll a rock up a mountain; it is, as Martin Buber points us, "To set out in the direction of the divine."

In the early Christian church, the primary time for the celebration of baptism was late in the night before the dawn of Easter morning. In a dramatic moment in the liturgy, the candidates faced west and renounced the powers of sin, the world, the flesh, and the devil. They then were invited to turn east toward the rising sun, the direction in which early Christians prayed. One of the famous bishops of the early church, Basil, told us the reason Christians faced east: "Few know that this is because we are seeking the ancient fatherland, which God planted in Eden, toward the east."[15]

Questions for Reflection

1. What does the word "sin" evoke in your mind or your memory? Does that idea of sin conform to the idea of separation and broken relationship discussed in this chapter?

---

15. Basil the Great, "On the Holy Spirit" 27.66, quoted in Louth, *Ancient Christian Commentary*, 54.

2. Brené Brown discusses a difference between shame and guilt. How do you understand the difference between these two things?

3. Have you experienced both the urge toward goodness and the pull towards disconnection or the will to selfishness in your life? How? When?

4. Can we ever get ourselves back to the garden without the assistance of God or a "higher power"?

4

Returning

You only know where you are by memorizing where you came from.

—Nainoa Thompson

Being lost is simply a failure of memory.

—Margaret Atwood

The stories we read in the early chapters of Genesis emerged out of basic human experience. The ancient Jewish writers sought to answer the big questions as to where we and the world came from. They also believed that human beings were essentially good—created in the image of God, with inherent dignity and purpose. And yet, they, like us, knew that all is not right with the world. We experience personal disconnection with other people and with God. Beyond that, we see communal and global evil around us. As we said in the previous chapter, human beings long for a life of harmony between the planet, one another, and God. We want to get back to the garden. We need to find our way home.

In the first chapter, I said finding our way requires us to orient ourselves to where we are and where we came from. We want to find our identity by placing ourselves within a history and a family. We want to know who our tribe is. We want to know what's in our DNA. That desire is at the heart of the narratives of the Bible. The ancient storytellers of the Hebrew Bible wanted to let their readers know who they were, where they came from, and where they were headed.

The stories I tell in this chapter aren't anywhere near the entire sweep of the Hebrew Bible. For Christians, these central traditions form the foundation of our understanding of the Jesus story and the Christian way. These stories, while based in history, have a mythic component. They provide meaning for our lives as they have for countless millions throughout time. We are fellow travelers with these ancient Jewish people. We can find our own place and our own direction within the stories they tell as we make them our own.

At the Great Vigil of Easter, as our congregation gathers around the fire, we recall the story of ancient Israel. We remember that we, too, are descendants of our Jewish ancestors. Our Christian story is first and foundationally a Jewish story. On that night as we prepare to celebrate the greatest Christian feast, we remember that once we were not a people; we were scattered everywhere and have come from many places. Now we are God's people. This is the night we remember who we are.

Our Father Was a Wanderer

Other ancient religions sought to reach out to the gods to gain a sense of control over their lives in an often-chaotic world. The religion of Israel saw God as searching for humankind, as much as human beings were seeking after God—as if God continues to call out trying to find us, as God did to the first human hiding in the garden: "Adam, where are you?"

As I write this chapter I'm travelling through the West Bank in the Holy Land, around Hebron in the Judean Mountains. Thousands of years ago in this place the Bible tells us a man named Abram and his wife Sarai entertained three visitors who promised them that they would soon have a son. In the centuries that followed, this man would come to be revered as the father of Jews, Christians, and Muslims. His story is central to the story of the Bible. He was born far from Hebron, in the Fertile Crescent in Mesopotamia in a place called Ur. Why did they wind up in the place we call the Holy Land?

As the book of Genesis relates the story, many generations had passed since the first man and woman left Eden. Abram was a nomadic herdsman who worshipped the gods of his people. The remarkable thing about Abram is that we never hear that he was a man who was particularly dissatisfied with his life, or an ardent spiritual seeker, or especially talented, or anything else that might set him apart. We simply are told God reached out to him.

So why Abram? Maybe he just listened more closely than other people and heard the still, small voice of God calling within him and he was daring enough or crazy enough to go where God asked and do as God wanted him to do. Here's how Genesis begins Abram's story:

> The Lord said to Abram, "Leave your land, your family, and your father's household for the land that I will show you. I will make you a great nation and will bless you. I will make your name respected, and you will be a blessing. I will bless those who bless you,
>
> Those who curse you I will curse; all the families of earth will be blessed because of you."
>
> Abram left just as the Lord told him.[1]

Many centuries later in the New Testament, the apostle Paul will say the faith of this first ancestor of the Jewish people was the one thing that singled him out. He listened to God and acted in faith. Abram, his son Isaac, and his grandson Jacob (who would be renamed Israel) were not qualitatively better, holier, or more heroic than anyone else. Faith was the defining factor and the apostle Paul says it's that way for us as well—but we'll discuss that later.

---

1. Gen. 12:1–4a, CEB.

As the story in Genesis continues, God invites Abram into a special sort of relationship called a covenant. In the ancient world, since there were no established legal practices for enforcing agreements between people, making a covenant was a way to make an agreement. The people making the covenant would rather dramatically split an animal or animals in half and then walk between the two pieces declaring that if they did not uphold their part of the bargain, the same thing would happen to them. It's pretty graphic. I guess it was meant to be. In fact, entering into such an agreement was called "cutting a covenant."

According to the story, God promises to give Abram a fruitful land and many descendants. Abram didn't have a son of his own and was going to make the son of one of his servants his heir. Even though Abram and his wife were well beyond childbearing years, God asks Abram to believe that God would do as God promised:

> But the word of the Lord came to [Abram], "This man shall not be your heir; no one but your very own issue shall be your heir." He brought him outside and said, "Look toward heaven and count the stars, if you are able to count them." Then he said to him, "So shall your descendants be." And he believed the Lord; and the Lord reckoned it to him as righteousness.
>
> Then he said to him, "I am the Lord who brought you from Ur of the Chaldeans, to give you this land to possess." But he said, "O Lord God how am I to know that I shall possess it?" He said to him, "Bring me a heifer three years old, a female goat three years old, a ram three years old, a turtledove, and a young pigeon." He brought him all these and cut them in two, laying each half over against the other; but he did not cut the birds in two. And when birds of prey came down on the carcasses, Abram drove them away.
>
> As the sun was going down, a deep sleep fell upon Abram, and a deep and terrifying darkness descended upon him.
>
> When the sun had gone down and it was dark, a smoking fire pot and a flaming torch passed between these pieces. On that day the Lord made a covenant with Abram, saying, "To your descendants

I give this land, from the river of Egypt to the great river, the river Euphrates.[2]

Notice it's God, represented by the fire and smoke, who passes through the pieces of the animal. Abram doesn't walk between them. In fact, Abram doesn't make any pledge that he will do anything for God except to believe God will do for him what God has promised.

The kind of covenant God makes with Abram is more than a simple contract. Every time I pull up to the parking lot at my gym I take a little card from the machine before the gate opens. In effect, every time I do that I'm entering into a contract. "This contract limits our liability" is printed in bold letters and there follows a whole list of stipulations in exceptionally fine print about what the parking company is not liable for if I choose to park my car in their garage. Contracts define and specify precisely what obligations each party agrees to. They are meant to create sharp lines of responsibility. In a contract you relate to somebody else as a means of exchange. It determines who is responsible for what and is limited in duration. When I leave the parking lot at the gym, my contract with the parking company ends.

A covenant like the one God makes with Abram is different. It's about ongoing relationship, sort of like marriage, which we often refer to as a covenant. When two people marry, they vow to be in an ongoing relationship with one another. You probably know the classic wedding vows. Each person pledges to love, comfort, honor, and keep the other in sickness and in health, forsaking all others, and to be faithful as long as they both shall live. There are no bold letters limiting liability, no small print. It is an open-ended commitment to another person whatever may come, and to do so forever.

While I sometimes can understand the need some couples have for a prenuptial agreement, it always makes me nervous. It seems as though an asterisk is being placed on the vows stipulating when they don't apply.

---

2. Gen. 15:4–12, 17–18.

Worse still might be couples who seek to make vows to one another "as long as love shall last." Ethicist Zygmunt Bauman[3] discusses two tendencies in relationships. The first he calls "fixing." I will enter into a relationship with you if I know exactly what I'm getting into and how we will get out of it if we need to. The other end of the spectrum he calls "floating." I will love you as long as we both need and want to be in this relationship, but life changes. The question in the titles of songs by Carole King and later Amy Winehouse may haunt people in such relationships: "Will you still love me tomorrow?" Neither "fixing" nor "floating" are what true love is all about. Rather, love just says yes to joining with a fellow traveler on the journey into the future. I will be there. I won't abandon you.

That is the kind of relationship God seeks to have with Abram and all his descendants after him. In fact, later in the story, when the people of Israel wander away from following God, the prophets call them back, telling them that although they have been like a faithless wife, God is faithful and wants to restore them to the relationship he always wanted to have with them.

God makes Abram a promise as part of the covenant: he will father offspring as numerous as the stars. When I remember again the night sky in the desert, the stars were beyond counting. And God says Abram won't just be the father of one nation, but of many. When Abram accepts God's invitation, he receives a new name to go with his new identity as God's chosen, as one who no longer is a wanderer but a pilgrim on his way to a new land that God will also give him. The name is Abraham—ancestor of a multitude.

Ancient Israel saw in the story of Abraham the foundation of their identity as chosen by God. It was their status as children of Abraham that gave them a sense of who they were and a destiny as God's people. Instead of testing DNA to determine their place in the world as we might do today, the Jewish people told a story about what made them unique from all the other nations of the world. In later times the people of Israel would recite their ancient history and teach these stories to their children

---

3. Bauman, *Postmodern Ethics*, 98–99.

as a way of remembering who they were. The Jewish feasts all convey a sense of remembering a communal past that helped to forge their identity as a people.

An even more tangible way of remembering the covenant relationship with God came through the physical and indelible sign God gives Abraham: circumcision. "This is my covenant that you and your descendants must keep: Circumcise every male. You must circumcise the flesh of your foreskins, and it will be a sign of the covenant between us. . . Your flesh will embody my covenant as an enduring covenant."[4] We might think this is kind of primitive, not to mention painful. But in our culture, we seal our bodies with tattoos or piercings. A tattoo may very well serve the same purpose to provide a physical reminder of a relationship, of an event, or to display to the world who you are. It's especially painful when someone prematurely tattoos the name of their boyfriend or girlfriend on their arm only to break up later. For Abraham, circumcision was the physical sign of God's claim on him and his children for all future generations; "No going back," God says. "You are mine."

We might ask how women fit into this very male-oriented covenant. I think we have to acknowledge that this tradition comes from a patriarchal cultural experience. Nevertheless, God makes a promise to Sarai as well as to Abraham. God says to Abraham, "As for your wife Sarai, you will no longer call her Sarai. Her name will now be Sarah. I will bless her and even give you a son from her. I will bless her so that she will become nations, and kings and peoples will come from her."[5] She too has a name change. Sarah means the royal mother of nations. The fact that God's covenant refers to the bearing of children makes both Sarah and Abraham partners in God's covenant plan for the future.[6]

The ancient Jewish tradition understood being children of Abraham in a very narrow way; that is, a group of people who believed they were physical descendants of Abraham. This belief set the Jewish people apart from their neighbors, especially in the time of the exile in Babylon. Being

---

4. Gen. 17:10–11, 13b, CEB.

5. Gen. 17:15–16, CEB.

6. Sohn, *Abraham's Covenant*.

people who shared the story of common ancestry, who kept the same divine law, and who were marked by the covenant sign of circumcision all helped them maintain distinctiveness while they were far away from their homeland.

Yet a new way of understanding God's promises emerges in the prophets' visions in the Hebrew Bible. In fact, it seems that the experience in Babylon not only strengthened the identity of the Jewish people, it helped them see their vocation as leading other peoples of the world into relationship with God. As the people start to re-make their lives in the land of Israel after their return, the prophet Isaiah offers this vision: "It is not enough, since you are my servant, to raise up the tribes of Jacob and to bring back the survivors of Israel. Hence I will also appoint you as a light to the nations so that my salvation may reach to the ends of the earth."[7]

At the very end of the book, the prophet envisions God's people bringing all the nations together as God begins a new work of recreating the world: "As the new heavens and the new earth that I'm making will endure before me, says the Lord, so your descendants and your name will endure, From month to month and from Sabbath to Sabbath, all humanity will come to worship me, says the Lord."[8] The promise given to Abraham is far greater and better than Abraham's descendants had imagined. That's the great good news of the long arc of the Bible's story. It's good news for Abraham's children—and that includes even you and me.

The covenant with Abraham isn't the only covenant in the Bible. Abraham's grandson Jacob, later named Israel, would have many sons. One of them was a remarkable young man named Joseph. Through the twists and turns of a story found at the end of Genesis, the family winds up in Egypt where they become enslaved by Pharaoh.[9]

Of course, the oppression of one people by another isn't news. It seems that out of fear, suspicion, and a will to power, we humans tend to see

---

7. Isa. 49:6, CEB.

8. Isa. 66:22–23, CEB.

9. The story of Joseph and his brothers makes a sort of novella at the end of Genesis. I encourage you to read it—Gen. 37–50. It is one of the classic stories in the whole Bible.

ourselves and our "tribe" as unique and privileged. It's not only that we want to know our place in the world. We seek to make it secure by giving ourselves the advantage over others. We don't have to look farther than our own backyard. I'm reminded of the stories of the race and class divides in the United States, how the legacy of African American slavery still poisons our society. Think about how Japanese people were feared as a security threat in the Second World War, or how Muslims are sometimes looked at with suspicion in our day, or the rising tide of anti-Semitism.

It is no surprise the dominant Egyptian culture saw the Hebrew immigrants as a security threat and placed them in bondage where they lived as slaves for many generations. God once again reached out and found a man who, like Abraham, was able to see and hear in a way other people couldn't. His name was Moses.

Exodus, Wandering, and Returning

In the middle of the Sinai Desert, a fugitive was working as a sheepherder for his father-in-law. He discovered a strange sight—a bush was on fire but it didn't burn up. If that wasn't strange enough, the man heard the voice of God coming from that burning bush. But who was this guy and how did he get there?

According to Exodus, the second book in the Bible, Pharaoh wanted to decrease the surplus population of Hebrew slaves so he made a rule that all the male babies should be killed as soon as they were born. One woman hid her newborn boy until she couldn't hide him any longer. She put him in a basket and placed him in the Nile River hoping somebody would find him. Pharaoh's own daughter found the boy and took him into her household and named him Moses.

It seems Moses had a passion for justice at an early age. One day he saw an Egyptian beating a Hebrew slave. Moses took the law into his own hands and killed the Egyptian. Knowing he was going to be found out, Moses fled Egypt and lived in the desert—that's where he sees the burning bush. God commands him to take his shoes off because the place where God reaches out to Moses is holy. In many stories of the Bible, wherever God meets us is holy ground.

God reminds Moses that God's people are living in slavery. God will not stand this oppression any longer and he wants Moses to be a partner, to help God free the people. Moses is not exactly a likely candidate for the mission. He is afraid to go; he stutters, he's unsure of himself. And yet, he's the one God chooses. In the end Moses goes to Pharaoh and takes his brother Aaron along as his support.

As the story continues, Pharaoh isn't so eager to let the slaves go free. Slave labor is a big economic benefit, so why would he let them go just because a guy heard a voice from a burning bush in the desert? But God sends several signs the Bible calls "plagues" to help convince Pharaoh he would be better off without the children of Israel. After each plague, Pharaoh still refuses to let them go, until this last terrifying one takes place.

> Moses said, "This is what the Lord says: At midnight I'll go throughout Egypt. Every oldest child in the land of Egypt will die, from the oldest child of Pharaoh who sits on his throne to the oldest child of the servant woman by the millstones, and all the first offspring of the animals. Then a terrible cry of agony will echo through the whole land of Egypt unlike any heard before or that ever will be again. But as for the Israelites, not even a dog will growl at them, at the people, or at their animals. By this, you will know that the Lord makes a distinction between Egypt and Israel. Then all your officials will come down to me, bow to me, and say, 'Get out, you and all your followers!' After that I'll leave." Then Moses, furious, left Pharaoh.
>
> The Lord said to Moses, "Pharaoh won't listen to you so that I can perform even more amazing acts in the land of Egypt." Now Moses and Aaron did all these amazing acts in front of Pharaoh, but the Lord made Pharaoh stubborn so that he didn't let the Israelites go from his land.[10]

That night, all the Hebrew people gather inside their homes and are told to eat a lamb and place the blood of the lamb on their doorposts. When the angel of death passes through Egypt on that night, killing all

---

10. Exod. 11:1–10, CEB.

the firstborn sons of the Egyptians, those with the blood of the lamb on their doorposts would be saved, passed over, from death. In future generations, that meal would be celebrated again and again, year in and year out, as a solemn commemoration—a feast called Passover. God remembered the covenant with Abraham and his children. That was the last night they were slaves in Egypt. From then on they would have a new identity.

The people left town in a hurry. And they went into the wilderness and headed out for the land God had promised their ancestor Abraham— the place we call today the Holy Land. The story from the book of Exodus tells us God directed them on their journey. But then Pharaoh realized the economic implications of letting the people go free and he sent his army to get them back. Israel had gotten to the edge of the sea[11] when Pharaoh's powerful army showed up with all their war horses and chariots and charioteers. Here they were, a bunch of unprotected fugitive slaves trying to make their way to freedom. The sea on one side, Pharaoh's military might on the other—it seemed like there was no way out. But God made a way where there seemed to be no way. The Bible recounts that God split the water open for his people to walk through. Once they got to the other side, and once Pharaoh's army moved in on them, God brought the waters back, drowning and destroying all the military might of Egypt's army.

But that wasn't the end of it. God sought to form this group of ex-slaves into his people and it took forty years in the desert to do it. During that time God provided them with bread from heaven called manna and quail to eat, and gives them water gushing from a rock when they were thirsty. We also hear that they complained a lot. They looked back to where they had been. Sometimes, even being slaves in Egypt seemed like a better alternative than going forward into the uncertainty of the future. During that time, as the story goes, God made another covenant with them at the same place where God first met Moses: Mount Sinai. It is here that God begins to give a law, really a way of life, to Israel.

---

11. If you know the story you might have heard of this as the Red Sea, but the Bible actually uses the term *Yam Suph*, or Reed Sea. Probably the Bible is simply referring to a large body of water filled with rushes and reeds rather than the name of a specific body of water.

> The Lord called to [Moses] from the mountain, "This is what you should say to Jacob's household and declare to the Israelites: You saw what I did to the Egyptians, and how I lifted you up on eagles' wings and brought you to me. So now, if you faithfully obey me and stay true to my covenant, you will be my most precious possession out of all the peoples, since the whole earth belongs to me. You will be a kingdom of priests for me and a holy nation. These are the words you should say to the Israelites."
>
> So Moses came down, called together the people's elders, and set before them all these words that the Lord had commanded him. The people all responded with one voice: "Everything that the Lord has said we will do." Moses reported to the Lord what the people said.[12]

The writers of Exodus remember God's gentle love for Israel as a mother eagle caring for her children and bringing them to her. This may seem like favoritism. Why does God like them best? Yet notice that even here Israel's vocation isn't for its own sake. They receive the particular commands of the lifestyle God will give them as priests. In other words, they are the ones who will mediate God's dream to all humanity. They will be a demonstration project of the way God seeks for all people to live.

God's presence at Sinai is both intimate and terrifying. God shows up in the midst of thunder, lighting, and clouds. The people are asked to stay away from the mountain because God's holy presence is so awesome, mysterious, and powerful, and at the same time, intimate. Annie Dillard discusses this sense of the awesome power of the divine as she reflects on the power of the natural world all around us. But then she also cautions us:

> Does anyone have the foggiest idea what sort of power we so blithely invoke? Or, as I suspect, does no one believe a word of it? The churches are children playing on the floor with their chemistry sets, mixing up a batch of TNT to kill a Sunday morning. It is madness to wear ladies' straw hats and velvet hats to church; we should all be wearing crash helmets. Ushers should issue life preservers and signal flares; they should lash us to our pews. For the sleeping god may

---

12. Exod. 19:3b–8, CEB.

wake someday and take offense, or the waking god may draw us out to where we can never return.[13]

That sort of divine awe, traditionally called the fear of God, is something we need to recapture. The one we worship is the Lord of the universe who is beyond our comprehension, the creator of all things. That's pretty powerful. And yet this is the same God who sees oppression and rescues the oppressed, who lifts up the lowly. As the old African American expression puts it, "God sits high, but He looks low."

The "waking god," as Dillard puts it, brought Israel out of Egypt and they could never return the way they came, they could never be who they once were. When you and I encounter the God of Sinai, we should know we will be changed by the experience.

When God speaks to Moses God gives him the centerpiece of the law that is to govern their lives, what we call the Ten Commandments. Then the story continues with commandments about how to conduct worship and the keeping of the Sabbath and festivals and making a tent where God's presence can travel right along with the people on their journey. In the midst of this, Moses sacrifices oxen. He reads the scroll of the covenant that God is making with the people, asking them to obey all the laws he has given them. The people say they will be in relationship with God and obey all these things he has asked them to do. Then he takes some of the blood of the oxen and sprinkles the people with it and says, "This is the blood of the covenant that the Lord now makes with you on the basis of all these words."[14]

The law God gives to Moses in the story defines the way that the Jewish people live out their unique relationship with God. As the rest of the early books of the Bible unfold, there are commandments that inform their daily lives, to act justly with one another, to care for the land, to reverence God. All these things, as I have said, form a particular lifestyle to help make the world right again, to bring them back into the right relationship with God that humanity lost through a desire to go it alone in the

---

13. Dillard, *The Abundance*, 253.
14. Exod. 24:8, CEB.

wilderness. For the ancient people of the Bible, the law was a map to help them find their way home.

The law gave them a way to make all of life holy. All the commandments reminded them who they were and to whom they belonged. Even as they lived as a minority community of exiles in Babylon they were able to say: "Your statutes have been like songs to me wherever I have lived as a stranger."[15] The way of life the law gave the Jewish people was what held them together. They saw the law as the way God intended for human beings to live. It didn't constrain their freedom, it enabled them to live more freely as their creator had intended from the beginning before we lost our way.

The journey through the wilderness is not all roses. There are ups and downs and turns in the road. The people often turn away from God even as they journey to the Promised Land, but in time they come to the end of their wandering at the edge of a small river called the Jordan. On the other side will be the place they have been journeying toward for so long. Moses, who has led them all this way will not join them. He looks out over the Promised Land, but he will not get there with them.

So many other stories fill the pages of the Hebrew Bible. The people would take control of the land, would eventually desire to have a king, just like all the other nations around them, and would look to the reigns of David and his son Solomon as the golden age of Israel's life. The city of Jerusalem would become the center of their world, and above all the temple would become the great touchstone of Jewish identity and memory and would strongly influence the development of the Christian tradition and our spiritual language. Yet above all, the tale of slavery, freedom, wandering, and homecoming became the central spiritual event in the life of ancient Israel and of the language of Christian tradition as we will see in the following chapters.

A New Exodus

As we discussed in the last chapter, the Babylonian Empire destroyed Jerusalem in the summer of 587/86 BCE and ransacked the temple. They

---

15. Ps. 119:54, The Book of Common Prayer, 1979.

took the best and brightest of Jewish society into captivity. During their exile, the people returned to the story of exodus from Egypt as the source of comfort and hope. They came to understand their experience as a judgement on their wandering away from the path the Lord had given them to walk. The exile became for them a way to renew their relationship with God, to once again go through the experience of the desert and return to the Lord.

> The Lord says—who makes a way in the sea
> and a path in the mighty waters,
> who brings out chariot and horse,
> army and battalion;
> they will lie down together and will not rise;
> they will be extinguished, extinguished like a wick.
> Don't remember the prior things;
> don't ponder ancient history.
> Look! I'm doing a new thing;
> now it sprouts up; don't you recognize it?
> I'm making a way in the desert,
> paths in the wilderness.[16]

The exile in Babylon and return to Jerusalem forged the identity of the Jewish people in a new way. It was in this time that the law that formed their common life was codified and ancient oral traditions and memories written down into the form we might recognize today.

This brings us to a question: how much of all these stories are historical? In the end we don't know for sure. There is little historical or archeological evidence for the patriarch Abraham, his son Isaac, or grandson Jacob (Israel) and yet these are the traditions handed on through the generations. The slaves who left Egypt may very well have forged their kinship in the crucible of shared suffering rather than that of a common ancestry. Those slaves may have enlisted more people who shared a similar oppression when they entered the Promised Land. While we cannot be sure of the historical facts of this ancient history, we can be sure that

---

16. Isa. 43:16–19, CEB.

these remembered experiences formed the Jewish people in their Holy Land, in their holy city, and in the temple where they experienced the presence of the living God in their midst and they are our ancestors in the faith.

We now need to take up another theme from Israel's spiritual journey—one we have touched on already. The ideas of sacrifice and the temple were part and parcel of the life of the Jewish people. These themes formed the early Christian understanding of Jesus's death and resurrection and gave vocabulary to Christians as they came to articulate a faith and vision for God's future.

Sacrifice, Atonement, and Temple

As soon as they are exiled from Eden, Cain and Abel, the sons of the first humans, make sacrificial offerings. Everywhere in early human cultures there was a desire to offer sacrifices to the divine. Why is that? Offering animals or the produce of the earth, or even human life itself, served as an invitation to relationship, a hope that the gods would not be silent. Often sacrifice was intended to appease their anger. Ancient people wanted to know the gods were on their side and a sacrifice was a primal way of inviting God or the gods to be with them, to forgive them for what they had done, and to restore them again, to make things right. Sacrifice was the answer to their primal dis-ease with the way the world was. That is what we mean by the term "atonement": to reconcile ourselves with each other and God—to make us one.

One of the greatest stories of sacrifice appears in Genesis chapter 22:1–19. Remember Abraham, our father? God finally gives him and Sarah a son named Isaac. Then God says to Abraham, "Take your son, your only son, whom you love, Isaac, and go to the land of Moriah. Offer him up as an entirely burned offering there on one of the mountains that I will show you."

In a dramatic unfolding of the story, the Bible tells us Abraham takes his son up the mountain. Isaac sees the wood for the fire, but wonders where the lamb for the burnt offering is. "God will provide," Abraham tells him. When they get to the top of the mountain, Abraham binds his son to the altar of sacrifice and just in the moment he is about to wield the cleaver to sacrifice him an angel calls out, "Abraham, Abraham."

"I'm here," he says, stopping short from inflicting the fatal blow.

"Don't stretch out your hand against that young man and don't do anything to harm him. Now I know you revere God and would not hold back your son, your only son from me." Just then, he sees a ram caught in a thicket and Abraham offers it to the Lord.

The story is often called the sacrifice of Isaac; more correctly, in the Jewish tradition it is called the *akidah*, the binding of Isaac, because in the end no human sacrifice is required. God uses this event to test Abraham's faith.

Clearly, human sacrifice was not uncommon in the ancient world and perhaps through this story the Jewish people indicated their separation from the other nations by not offering human sacrifice. It also seems that when they would offer rams and lambs as sacrificial offering, they would remember that God provided the sacrifice for Abraham and ransomed his son, their ancestor, by means of an animal.

As we have seen, sacrifice ratified the covenant relationship between God and the people. It served as a reminder of their ongoing relationship with one another. The wisdom of sacrifice in ancient Israel was also to stipulate what was sufficient for the sacrifice. That is, once you offer what the law prescribes, then right relationship is restored. For example, the offering of a lamb as a sacrifice for sin as prescribed in the law did in fact restore the relationship with God.

This is seen in the description of the ritual on the Day of Reconciliation or Atonement (see Leviticus 16). Annually, around the time of the new year, the covenant would be renewed with a special sacrificial rite in which the high priest would enter the presence of the Lord. The Bible remembers this as having happened even in the wilderness. The tabernacle, the tent where Israel experienced God's presence dwelling with them, was seen as the symbolic place where God dwelt with the people. Later, that special place continued to exist in the temple in Jerusalem.

Within the temple there was an inner area called the *devir*, or the holy of holies. The high priest would enter it only on the Day of Reconciliation and he would take with him a bull, which he would offer for his own sins and those of his family, and two goats. One of them would be sacrificed, and the other he would lay his hands on and confess the sins of all the people for the past year. Then that goat would be led out into the wilderness. The high priest would place on that goat all the sin and shame of God's people and it would symbolically take their place wandering in the wilderness away from God, while the people would be restored to right relationship. Whatever separated them from God no longer was remembered.

The place where the temple stood has traditionally (maybe symbolically) been associated with Mount Moriah, where Abraham bound Isaac and where God provided the ram for sacrifice. So there it is that Solomon erected the first temple and then where the temple was rebuilt after the exile in Babylon as the place where the rams of sacrifice and the scapegoats were offered to the Lord for the sins of the people.

On a cool Sunday morning I stand on the Mount where the temple once stood. It is a vast pavement. I can only imagine what the temple must have been like after the maniacal monarch Herod the Great completed his building project. The first-century Jewish historian Josephus tells us the white stone reflected light so brilliantly that from far away people thought it was a snow-covered mountain. The gold Herod used to gild the temple was so bright you would have to avert your eyes from the brilliance.

Today, all that's left is the platform. Down below stands the western retaining wall where Jews remember the temple and pray daily toward the Holy of Holies. On the Temple Mount stands the Al-Aqsa Mosque and the Dome of the Rock—the place where most scholars believe the holiest place of the temple once stood. But nothing remains of the once-beautiful temple, the center of the earth, where God once met God's people.

Roman legions laid siege to Jerusalem after a period of tumultuous conflict between the Empire of Rome and the Jewish people. In 70 CE, the Roman general Titus finally had the temple destroyed on the ninth of the Hebrew month of Av, which would have been August 10 on our Western calendars. Eerily, it was the same day the Babylonians destroyed the first temple.

The destruction of the temple ended the sacrificial system of the Jewish people, apart from a few brief attempts to restore it after the temple was destroyed. It would remain for the Jewish people to make sense of their relationship with God after this devastating event. How could sin be forgiven without a temple? One answer to that question emerges in the new movement of a rabbi named Jesus.

The Words of the Prophets

While the temple in Jerusalem and the capital of the monarchy following the kingly line of David are central in the history of Israel, alternative voices emerge from the margins of this story: the words of the prophets. While the political structures of Israel and the priestly structures of the temple and the sacrificial system all lent themselves to stability and predictability, the prophets give voice to the wild, unpredictable God who is about to do a new thing. They call Israel to remember both their roots in the wilderness, where God led them and formed them as a people; and that the center of their relationship with God is summed up in Micah's denunciation of the sacrificial system:

> Will the Lord be pleased with thousands of rams,
> with ten thousands of rivers of oil?
> Shall I give my firstborn for my transgression,
> the fruit of my body for the sin of my soul?"
> He has told you, O mortal, what is good;
> and what does the Lord require of you
> but to do justice, and to love kindness,
> and to walk humbly with your God?[17]

While sacrifice is central to forgiveness, so is living into the right relationship between people and with God envisioned in the law. The Psalm writers often turn to this idea:

> "Hear, O my people, and I will speak,
> O Israel, I will testify against you.
> "I am God, your God.
> Not for your sacrifices do I rebuke you;

---

17. Mic. 6:7–8.

your burnt offerings are continually before me.
I will not accept a bull from your house,
or goats from your folds.
For every wild animal of the forest is mine,
the cattle on a thousand hills.
I know all the birds of the air,
and all that moves in the field is mine.
"If I were hungry, I would not tell you,
for the world and all that is in it is mine.
Do I eat the flesh of bulls,
or drink the blood of goats?
Offer to God a sacrifice of thanksgiving,
and pay your vows to the Most High.
Call on me in the day of trouble;
I will deliver you, and you shall glorify me."[18]

So the prophetic tradition emerges as one where sacrifice is less important than right acting, following the commands of God particularly in justice-making in our relations with one another.

This of course goes back to what we have been saying all along. The thrust of the story of the people of Israel is God's desire to enter into a relationship with human beings, and God's invitation for us to live in accord with our truest selves. Indeed, it was this sense of living righteously in accordance with the Torah that enabled the Jewish people to survive the destruction of not one, but two temples. What did the Lord truly require? "To do justice, love kindness and walk humbly with God," as Adam did in the cool of the evening.

Questions for Reflection

1. Annie Dillard writes: "Does anyone have the foggiest idea what sort of power we so blithely invoke? Or, as I suspect, does no one believe a word of it? . . . For the sleeping god may wake someday

---

18. Ps. 50:7–15.

and take offense, or the waking god may draw us out to where we can never return." Have we lost this sense of the power of the divine presence in our day? Where might we discover it? Where might the "waking god" be calling you to journey?

2. In the book of Genesis God calls out: "Adam, where are you?" How can the covenants God gives to Abraham and Moses be ways God seeks to reach out to human beings?

3. The stories of exodus, exile, wandering, and return are central to the story of the Bible. Many people have seen the stories of their experience in these biblical tales. Do you? How?

4. How can Christians understand these ancient tales of the Hebrew Scriptures as our "family stories"?

5

Jesus—The Way

One evening while on pilgrimage in the Holy Land I was exploring the Old City of Jerusalem with a few of my fellow pilgrims. We made our way through the checkpoint approaching the Western or Wailing Wall. I wasn't prepared for my reaction as I had my first glimpse of what remains of the ancient temple. I felt a mixture of overwhelming joy and tears all at once. It is nothing more than a retaining wall, but above, on the temple mount is the place where the Jewish people experienced the presence of God. Here Jesus walked and worshipped. Now I too went, washing my hands, covering my head with a yarmulke. I approached that place of prayer as have so many others who left their petitions on small pieces of paper tucked into the stones. As I touched the wall, adding my own prayers, the words of the psalmist flooded my mind:

> But you, O LORD, endure for ever,
> and your Name from age to age.
> You will arise and have compassion on Zion,
> for it is time to have mercy upon her;
> indeed, the appointed time has come.

For your servants love her very rubble,
and are moved to pity even for her dust.
For the Lord will build up Zion,
and his glory will appear.
He will look with favor on the prayer of the homeless;
he will not despise their plea.[1]

In that moment I understood the emotion the psalmist described as he beheld the ruins of the first temple. Jerusalem had been sacked by the Babylonians generations before this wall was built for the second temple. Babylon itself was then conquered by the Persians. It is under their rule that the people of Israel returned to rebuild their temple, their city, and their land, though still under foreign domination. Next followed the Greeks under Alexander the Great, and then the Seleucid Empire that came after him. There was only a brief period when Judea gained independence in the wake of the revolt of the Maccabees, recounted every year in the festival of Hanukkah. Finally, the might of imperial Rome swept in.

During the Roman occupation, the Jewish people looked to their tradition, especially the story of the Exodus, to sustain them. Would God return to the temple? Would God again free them from the hand of their oppressors? Jewish freedom fighters used tactics of violence and engaged in ongoing political and military uprisings until Rome finally crushed all resistance by sacking Jerusalem and razing the temple to the ground. Today faithful Jews still come to this place to mourn, to pray, and to hope. Has the glory of the Lord appeared? Has God been faithful? As a Christian, I see the faithfulness of God coming to the temple in a surprising way.

"For These Eyes of Mine Have Seen the Savior"

If I had been travelling the streets of Jerusalem around the time of the birth of Jesus, there would have been a steady flood of pilgrims, much as

---

1. Ps. 102:12–14, 16–17, The Book of Common Prayer, 1979, 731–32.

there still is today.[2] Herod the Great's glorious temple would have been the center of the city's life. Jews and Gentiles both would have filled the city streets.

One day, a man and a woman come with an infant in their arms, forty days after he was born. His parents bring him to the temple to give thanks and his mother will offer the small sacrifice of two turtledoves or pigeons the Torah commands for all women after giving birth. This is the offering of the poor, those who cannot afford to bring a lamb to sacrifice.

They may have already been in the city for a week preparing for this visit. I imagine them going up the steps near the southern gates. They may have already exchanged their coins for temple currency so that Roman money would not defile the house of God. They wash themselves in the ritual bath, the *mikveh*, to make themselves clean. They enter the dark and silent tunnels leading up to the Temple Mount, the walls illumined by the lamps, light glinting off the colorful designs decorating the vaulted ceilings above them.

They emerge into the brilliant light of the stone pavement in the courtyard. All around them they hear music and the chanting of psalms of praise. The air is full of the scents of incense, burning wood, and the roasting flesh of sacrifices. Yet even here, overshadowing the temple itself, are the towers of the Antonia Fortress, the place of the Roman legion's presence in Jerusalem. As they make their way to the place where they will offer the birds for the priests to sacrifice they meet a strange and wonderful old man. His piercing, dark eyes meet those of the young woman, Mary, and her husband, Joseph. The old man, Simeon, takes the child in his arms and sees something in him no one else detects. He seems both overjoyed and filled with sorrow all at once. He raises his voice in praise:

Lord, you now have set your servant free
to go in peace as you have promised;
For these eyes of mine have seen the Savior,
whom you have prepared for all the world to see:

---

2. Because of some miscalculations in dating, Jesus was probably born in about the year 4 BCE.

A Light to enlighten the nations,
and the glory of your people Israel.[3]

The child's parents are amazed. I can see why. It is not your normal greeting. Despite his joy, Simeon foresees something else, the sorrow this child and his mother both will face in the future. "A sword will pierce your soul," he tells her. Who could have known on that day, as happy new parents came to give thanks for their baby boy, that the future would bring such pain. Many years from now, only a short distance from this very place, the child will meet a humiliating death on a cross. But Simeon, if he sees this fate ahead, sees also that God is at work in the child whose name is Yeshua—Jesus; his name means "God rescues."

The people of Israel had been looking for God to return to the temple since they rebuilt it after they returned from Babylon. When would the glory of the Lord reappear as the psalmist asked? Simeon has eyes to see God's glory returning to the temple, not in clouds of majesty, but unassumingly, in a baby, the son of poor parents from the north country. Like Abraham, who listened carefully to hear God's promise, like Moses, who waited patiently to see a miracle—a bush burning but not consumed— God again appears silently to those who have eyes or ears to see or hear him coming.

Nearby, an old woman and prophetess named Anna also notices, realizing that through this baby God is about to redeem Israel. It is as if these two seers embody the hopes of all their ancestors. God has proven faithful, has suddenly come to the temple as the prophet Malachi proclaimed. God will finally make a way where there seemed to be no way, though not in the way they expected.

This story comes to us in Luke's Gospel, his account of the life of Jesus. He tells us that after these things this young mother, her husband, and the child return to their home in the north country of Galilee, to a little town of no more than two hundred people called Nazareth. There the child grows up. Luke remembers one other trip to Jerusalem at Passover when Jesus is twelve years old; he sits among the rabbis of Israel, listening

---

3. Luke 2:29–32, The Book of Common Prayer, 1979, 93.

to them and asking questions. He seems to be so engrossed that his parents can't find him for all the crowds. But apart from this we hear nothing more until he's grown. Except that his mother treasured all these things in her heart.[4]

Preparing the Way

We know little about the wild prophet of the Judean wilderness whose name was John. All four gospels tell us about him, although Luke tells a story about the birth of John in parallel to his story of the birth of Jesus. Luke says John was Jesus's cousin. Many scholars believe John was either a member of or at least influenced by the Jewish monastic community, the Essenes. They were radical separatists, forsaking the religious establishment of the temple and Jerusalem for a purer, more rigorous adherence to Jewish law.

The Gospels tell us John preached a new message that was disturbing to the status quo. He invited all who heard him to repent because God's kingdom has come near. Anyone who became a follower of his teaching was baptized in the Jordan River—not a simple repeatable ritual washing as was done in the temple, or even like the daily ritual cleaning the Essene monks performed in the mikveh. John's baptism signified a whole new beginning. To "repent" means to stop going in the direction you were headed and begin a new journey. Baptism in the Jordan signaled that new life.

Of course, the Jordan was a central symbol for the Jewish people. Remember it was here, after the long wandering in the wilderness for forty years, the Hebrew people finally entered the land of promise. To go into the waters of the Jordan and come out the other side was a clear symbol John's audience would have understood. God was about something new, remaking his people, showing them a new way. Mark, the earliest gospel writer, starts his story, "The beginning of the good news of Jesus Christ the Son of God." Mark tells us then about John the Baptizer, but

---

4. See Luke 2:22–52.

he's clear that John is preparing for someone else to arrive. One day, unexpectedly, he shows up.

Beloved

The River Jordan is not a grand expanse like the mighty Mississippi. It is a rather narrow, humble stream where John the Baptizer gathered crowds to listen to his teaching. Mark tells of Jesus coming to meet John.

> In those days Jesus came from Nazareth of Galilee and was baptized by John in the Jordan. And just as he was coming up out of the water, he saw the heavens torn apart and the Spirit descending like a dove on him. And a voice came from heaven, "You are my Son, the Beloved; with you I am well pleased."[5]

Mark tells his story with an economy of words and an urgent desire to convey his message; the word "immediately" appears some forty times as he tells his story. He conveys his message with few details, so we should pay attention to the ones he includes. First Jesus is baptized. Does he need to follow John as well? No, John says the one who comes after him, Jesus, is greater than he is. But Mark wants to say something to us his readers, the ones who want to know the good news about Jesus Christ the Son of God. If we want to follow him, then we too will follow him into the waters of baptism.

When Jesus comes out of the water the sky is torn open. As I imagine that day, I think of clouds moving across the sky and suddenly the sun breaks through as brilliant light explodes on the surface of the water. Why would Mark tell us that detail? At the end of the book of Isaiah, after the return from exile, the Jewish people wait for God's return, as did the psalmist, and Simeon and Anna in the temple. Isaiah cries out:

> O that you would tear open the heavens and come down,
> so that the mountains would quake at your presence—
> as when fire kindles brushwood

---

5. Mark 1:9–11.

and the fire causes water to boil—
to make your name known to your adversaries,
so that the nations might tremble at your presence!
When you did awesome deeds that we did not expect,
you came down, the mountains quaked at your presence.
From ages past no one has heard,
no ear has perceived,
no eye has seen any God besides you,
who works for those who wait for him.[6]

As Luke uses the story of Simeon to demonstrate God's nearly imperceptible coming to the temple, Mark too sees the coming of God not in earthquakes or fire, but in the one who will begin his ministry on the banks of Jordan in the backwater towns of Galilee. Mark also sees Jesus as God's anointed, the chosen one. Like a dove, the Spirit who moved over the waters at the dawn of creation in Genesis anoints and commissions Jesus. Here a new creation is beginning. We have been wandering in the wilderness since Adam and Eve left paradise, and the God who has been calling for us all this time and has been preparing for this day finally will lead us home by coming to us in the person of Jesus.

The voice of God calls out and points to this anointed one, calls him son, beloved. Again, Mark wants to tell us something about those of us who follow this Jesus. We too, as we come out of the water of baptism, are anointed with the spirit, called children of God, beloved. We will look at all that in detail later. Here Jesus is anointed, chosen for his mission. In Greek, the anointed one is called *Christos*, where we get our word "Christ"; in Hebrew, the messiah.

Wilderness

I stand listening to the complete silence of the Judean desert, the sun just beginning to rise, casting a purple and rose glow over the gentle curves of the barren mountains. The morning air is cold. I wrap myself in my scarf

---

6. Isa. 64:1–4.

and coat, wondering what it was like for Jesus in this very place. As soon as he was baptized, Mark, Luke, and Matthew[7] all tell us, Jesus came here after his baptism. "And the Spirit immediately drove him out into the wilderness. He was in the wilderness forty days, tempted by Satan; and he was with the wild beasts; and the angels waited on him."[8]

What did Jesus think and experience during that desert journey? This desert has called mystics and monastics over the generations to spend time here as Jesus did. I'm reminded of the vision quests young Native Americans take. They, too, fast in a wilderness and they may see wild beasts or even ancient spirits guiding them to understand their vocation. It seems Jesus too seeks clarity after his amazing experience at the Jordan. Where exactly is he headed?

While Mark gives us few details in his story, Matthew and Luke[9] tell us that the devil—Satan, the force of darkness—tempts Jesus, not unlike the serpent tempting Eve and Adam in the garden, using their human nature against them. In the wilderness, Jesus is tempted to indulge his physical passions by using his divine power to turn stones into bread. He's tempted to engage the power plays of the world by ruling the empires. He's tempted to use his power to get out of his situation as a human being and he's tempted to doubt himself. "*If* you are the son of God . . . ," Satan taunts him repeatedly. Despite, or maybe because of all these temptations, Jesus gains a clearer vision of the mission he has been given.

He leaves the wilderness and immediately begins his journey, calling ordinary people to follow him. And Satan? Luke ends his story of the wilderness with this chilling comment: the devil "departed from him until an opportune time." Jesus would not be done with self-doubt. He would not be done wondering if he, in fact, was the Son of God. He would not be done wondering whether his mission was in vain. He would have fears just like all

---

7. These three Gospels are referred to as "synoptics"—one eye, because they have a similar lens through which they tell the Jesus story. John, the fourth Gospel, tells his story in a different way. He includes details the others don't and doesn't refer to many stories the other gospel writers include.

8. Mark 1:12–13.

9. See Matt. 4:1–11 and Luke 4:1–13.

of us do. They would come crashing in on him, especially at the end of his life, as he knew the conflict with the powers of darkness was coming to its inevitable conclusion—the opportune time for the dark lord to do his worst.

Follow Me

The first words Jesus speaks in Matthew and Mark's accounts is an invitation to repent because the kingdom of God has come near. Mark adds that this is good news we should believe. In our culture, hearing someone asking us to repent doesn't sound like good news. We may imagine a person with a placard railing at us on a street corner and calling down vengeance from on high. "Turn or burn." "Hell, or heaven the choice is yours." But that is decidedly *not* what Jesus means by repentance, or even what the word itself means. The Greek word *metanoeite* is an imperative. It means change your heart; turn around. It can also mean to open your life to a new possibility.[10] Jesus invites his hearers, including us, to change direction. Maybe we've been wandering around trying to find our way. Jesus says, "Hey! God is doing something new. There is a whole new world order emerging even in the middle of this old one. Right now, the dark powers of empire, oppression and greed are all around us, but there's good news. Turn around—come this way and I'll show you the way forward." That's repentance Jesus-style.

Luke puts a slightly different slant on things, but it's pretty much the same idea. Jesus comes to the synagogue in his home town of Nazareth and he reads the words of the prophet Isaiah:

> The Spirit of the Lord is upon me,
> because the Lord has anointed me.
> He has sent me to preach good news to the poor,
> to proclaim release to the prisoners
> and recovery of sight to the blind,
> to liberate the oppressed,
> and to proclaim the year of the Lord's favor.

---

10. Cahill, *Desire*, 69–70.

He rolled up the scroll, gave it back to the synagogue assistant, and sat down. Every eye in the synagogue was fixed on him. He began to explain to them, "Today, this scripture has been fulfilled just as you heard it."[11]

The words of the prophet describe what God's kingdom is like: the poor have hope, the blind see—maybe those who can't see beyond the confines of the way the world currently is can see the possibility of a different future—the oppressed are freed, and a year of the Lord's favor is announced. In the Old Testament book of Leviticus, every fiftieth year was declared the jubilee year, in which all debts were forgiven, enslaved people were set free, and the mercy of God was especially apparent. Jesus says the kingdom of God is like the jubilee, only it never has to end.

When Jesus announces the kingdom of God, his first listeners in Galilee may have expected a revolution that would overthrow the power of Rome from their land. There had been many young insurgents before Jesus and more would follow. Yet the message of this young prophet was different. Not only did Jesus believe the battle against oppression was not to be fought with armed insurgence, he also believed that the battle was not simply against the political power of Rome. The coming kingdom sought to conquer the forces behind Rome, what Paul would later call principalities and powers working against God's best hope for us and the whole cosmos. Furthermore, Jesus believed that the kingdom was breaking into human history through his mission and he sought followers to join him in this "kingdom movement."[12] The great Christian writer C. S. Lewis puts it this way: "Enemy occupied territory—that is what the world is. Christianity is the story of how the rightful king has landed, you might say landed in disguise, and is calling us all to take part in a great campaign of sabotage."[13]

Jesus's invitation was both personal and communal. He challenged people to make a personal decision to be part of the Jesus movement, but

---

11. Luke 4:18–21, CEB.
12. Wright, "The Mission and Message," 41–42.
13. Lewis, *Mere Christianity*, 46.

it wasn't private. When I was a Pentecostal in my teenage years, I heard a song, "Me and Jesus, we got our own thing going." Nothing could be farther from what Jesus called his disciples to do. It isn't about me and Jesus. Of course, Jesus invited his first disciples to join a movement meant to transform each human heart, but also to change the world. That still is the same compelling invitation to you and me today.

Matthew, Mark, and Luke all relate some version of Jesus's invitation to his first disciples. They are fishermen, laborers who worked with their hands, going about their daily jobs when Jesus confronts them with the good news of his message. Jesus invites them to follow him and if they do, they will start fishing for people. They will be the ones who will extend his mission as they slowly grasp the impact of the journey on which they are about to embark. They seem to have said yes to him in a kind of covenant love. Believing him trustworthy, they left their nets and followed him.

John, who's fourth gospel views the story with a somewhat different lens, tells us that Andrew, Simon Peter's brother, and another disciple start following Jesus at the direction of John the Baptist. "When Jesus turned and saw them following, he asked, 'what are you looking for?' They said, 'Rabbi (which is translated Teacher), where are you staying?' He replied, 'Come and see.' "[14] The wrinkle John adds to the story helps us see that Jesus's invitation was not to an agenda, but to a journey, a way of life. Those first disciples didn't know all the details. They simply found the person and the words and deeds of Jesus so compelling that they opened their hearts and turned their whole lives around to follow him.

What's the Good News?

The Jesus we meet in the gospels shows us the way to the kingdom through his deeds and words. Let's explore some of the central elements of the Gospel stories to understand the good news of the kingdom of God as Jesus reveals it to us. Jesus's parables, his healings, his actions, and even the people he associates with give us a picture of the vision of God's future.

---

14. John 1:38–39a, CEB.

Stories of the Kingdom

Parables are the stories by which Jesus teaches us about the kingdom. The Greek word for parable means something cast beside some greater truth to make it clearer. The parables of Jesus are those stories of everyday people and life in his culture that help us understand a reality beyond what words can fully grasp.

Some parables are just a few lines, like this one: "The kingdom of heaven is like a mustard seed that someone took and planted in his field. It's the smallest of all seeds. But when it's grown, it's the largest of all vegetable plants. It becomes a tree so that the birds in the sky come and nest in its branches."[15] Of course, Jesus uses hyperbole here. Although a mustard seed is small, and mustard plants grow large, they hardly are trees. But Jesus wants us to see something amazing about the kingdom of God or, as Matthew calls it, the kingdom of Heaven. It starts small, with only a few people, but it grows larger as the seed is shared by others and planted in all kinds of soil. Living in California, I've seen fields of mustard growing up in the springtime. The little seeds start growing all over. Once it starts spreading it's nearly impossible to get rid of it. Once the tiny seed of hope for God's future is planted in our hearts and we share it, others will want to share the good news as well. Despite attempts to destroy the message of the Gospel it just keeps spreading. That's why Jesus's disciples need to be seed sowers, sharing the message of the kingdom through what we say and do and inviting other people to come join in the mission.

"He told them another parable: 'The kingdom of heaven is like yeast, which a woman took and hid in a bushel of wheat flour until the yeast had worked its way through all the dough.'"[16] Like so many of Jesus's parables, this one has lots packed into it—maybe like the dough itself. First God is like a woman baking bread—an upended view of how we normally think of God. Then the kingdom is like yeast working imperceptibly in the world and we don't always recognize it until we see the results.

---

15. Matt. 13:31–32, CEB.
16. Matt. 13:33, CEB.

One yeasty example is the movement to end apartheid in South Africa. It was only slowly—often with seemingly no results that the church, working along with other resistance movements, finally made headway to end the oppression of people of color. Then the whole system crashed in on itself. That is a sign of the kingdom at work in the world. It certainly wasn't the kingdom coming in its completion, but it was a sign of what can happen when Christians allow the yeast of God's kingdom loose in the world by their words and deeds. What's more, the kingdom grows silently in our hearts and will grow in us if we cultivate the ground. The yeast leavens our lives so that we can live abundantly by the power of Jesus who dwells in us through God's Spirit. As Robert Farrar Capon tells us:

What are the only responses you need to offer to the yeast in the dough? Well patience, for one thing. And possibly discernment—to be able to recognize when it (not you, please note) has done the job. And maybe a little vigilance to make sure impatient types don't talk you into despairing of the lump before its time comes. But no matter what you do, the yeast works anyway. At the most your responses advance your satisfaction, not its success.[17]

Matthew adds this line to his telling of the parables: "Jesus said all these things to the crowds in parables, and he spoke to them only in parables. This was to fulfill what the prophet spoke: I'll speak in parables; I'll declare what has been hidden since the beginning of the world."[18] The mustard seed and the yeast did not just pop into the world at the coming of Jesus. Matthew wants us to know that God has been at work in the world since the beginning of creation and has been seeking to restore the whole cosmos to God's original plan, to set God's image-bearers as priests in the temple of God's good creation. That is your vocation and mine—to become who we were created to be from the beginning of time.

Some of Jesus's parables are longer stories that engage our imaginations and sometimes make us ponder his meaning and even upset us. Take, for example, the story of laborers who start work at different times of the

---

17. Capron, *Kingdom, Grace, Judgment*, ch. 9.
18. Matt. 13:34–35, CEB; he refers to the first verses of Ps. 78.

day, but at the end are given the same wages. That's not fair, we might say; that's the logic of the kingdom, Jesus says. But let's focus on another story at the heart of Jesus's message and mission. I invite you to read the parable in its entirety, and then read it again.

> Jesus said, "A certain man had two sons. The younger son said to his father, 'Father, give me my share of the inheritance.' Then the father divided his estate between them. Soon afterward, the younger son gathered everything together and took a trip to a land far away. There, he wasted his wealth through extravagant living.
>
> "When he had used up his resources, a severe food shortage arose in that country and he began to be in need. He hired himself out to one of the citizens of that country, who sent him into his fields to feed pigs. He longed to eat his fill from what the pigs ate, but no one gave him anything. When he came to his senses, he said, 'How many of my father's hired hands have more than enough food, but I'm starving to death! I will get up and go to my father, and say to him, "Father, I have sinned against heaven and against you. I no longer deserve to be called your son. Take me on as one of your hired hands." ' So he got up and went to his father.
>
> "While he was still a long way off, his father saw him and was moved with compassion. His father ran to him, hugged him, and kissed him. Then his son said, 'Father, I have sinned against heaven and against you. I no longer deserve to be called your son.' But the father said to his servants, 'Quickly, bring out the best robe and put it on him! Put a ring on his finger and sandals on his feet! Fetch the fattened calf and slaughter it. We must celebrate with feasting because this son of mine was dead and has come back to life! He was lost and is found!' And they began to celebrate.
>
> "Now his older son was in the field. Coming in from the field, he approached the house and heard music and dancing. He called one of the servants and asked what was going on. The servant replied, 'Your brother has arrived, and your father has slaughtered the fattened calf because he received his son back safe and sound.' Then the older son was furious and didn't want to enter in, but his father came out and begged him. He answered his father, 'Look,

I've served you all these years, and I never disobeyed your instruction. Yet you've never given me as much as a young goat so I could celebrate with my friends. But when this son of yours returned, after gobbling up your estate on prostitutes, you slaughtered the fattened calf for him.' Then his father said, 'Son, you are always with me, and everything I have is yours. But we had to celebrate and be glad because this brother of yours was dead and is alive. He was lost and is found.' "[19]

What do you think and feel about this story? How does each character make you feel? Maybe you think the elder brother is right in his response. Maybe you think the father is crazy and unfair and the younger son is an outrageous slacker. All this may be true in the world as we know it. Jesus tells this story to open a new window on the logic of the kingdom. Who's in and who's out? There are all sorts of nuances; maybe some details jumped out at you. Let's focus on just a few elements.

The son takes his inheritance and leaves his father's house to go to a far-off country. Isn't that what humanity has done? We left Eden, the place of our unity with God, and went off to do our own thing. Human beings pretty much have said, "We can get along without you, God." But then things turn bad, all the things in which we have invested for our security: the good life, friends, a stable career, all go south quickly; things change, and we have to look at ourselves in the mirror. Who am I? What did I do? Where did I go? How did I wind up here?

The younger son has wandered off into the wilderness. He wishes he could eat pig slop. It can't get much lower than that. Then he "came to his senses." He knows he should try to go home, but how can he? He decides he can no longer be a son. He is not worthy. Like many people, the young man is ashamed of what he has become.

In chapter 3, I discussed Brené Brown's research on shame. I see the experience of the younger son in her definition of shame: "Shame is the fear of disconnection—it's fear that something we've done or failed to do, an ideal that we've not lived up to, or a goal that we've not accomplished

---

19. Luke 15:11–32, CEB.

makes us unworthy of connection. . . . I'm unlovable. I don't belong."[20] The younger son constructs an identity to allow him to go back to his father's house even though he doesn't belong. He will be a hired hand, disconnected from his father's love. Maybe that is the way a lot of people relate to God, trying to strike a bargain to make God love them, to feel somehow connected to a far-off and remote deity.

The son sets off on the journey home. Here's where the story gets amazing. While he is still far off the father sees him. That's the story of Israel. It's the story of God's people. While they are wandering, God claims them as God's own. Claims us. It's especially the story of Jesus, who isn't just a prophet, but God in the flesh coming to claim us. When the father reaches the younger son, he doesn't accept his unworthiness. He will not allow him ever to be disconnected. He will never just be a hired hand. "Dress him up in the clothes of my beloved son. Throw a lavish party, for this son of mine was dead and now is alive. He was lost and now he's found." He is worthy. He is connected. He is a son and not a slave. That is what the Bible calls grace—unmerited love and favor for you and for me, for everyone.

But what about justice? That's the voice of the elder son who seeks to shame his brother. I think that son is as much enslaved as the younger one. He is disconnected from his father as well. His relationship is as economic as if he had been a hired hand. "I have worked for you all my life and I haven't received anything from you," he says to his father, "but this son of *yours* wastes all your money, wanders far away, and he shows up and all is forgiven. What about punishment. What about restitution. What about *retribution?*"

In one sense the son's comments mirror the Pharisees', the Jewish religious leaders who saw themselves as devout keepers of God's law. Jesus often criticized their way of thinking—righteousness based on others being outsiders. But the father says to the elder son, "Come on in, son. Join the party. Can't you be happy that I have claimed this one back as well?"

---

20. Brown, *Daring Greatly*, 68.

It seems to me that the response of the elder brother is what hell is like. Hell is the state of those who will not allow themselves to be loved and forgiven, or, in their pride, will not participate in God's lavish party for all creation. I won't go in if *those* people are invited, even if it means I must stand outside in the cold for all eternity.

The kingdom of God is all about a lavish party. It's a great banquet for everyone where there is no shame or disconnection. All are welcome and all are forgiven. All we need to do is let go of whatever holds us back, to ask forgiveness for the ways we have messed up, and enter in. We must die to whatever pretensions prevent us—the illusions of our own righteousness are as deceptive as the illusions of our own unworthiness. You are worthy. You are welcome. You are beloved.

Actions Speak Louder than Words

Jesus's parables help us understand what the kingdom is like, but Jesus's actions—his healings and miracles—give us an even greater sense of the new reality that is breaking into our world. Throughout the gospels there are remarkable stories of what Jesus did: stories of paralytics walking, of the blind receiving sight, of the dead raised, of outsiders invited in—all signs that a future world is dawning even now.

All four gospels tell a version of a story involving feeding a huge group of hungry people, five thousand, in fact. I love John's version of the story.

Jesus looked up and saw the large crowd coming toward him. He asked Philip, "Where will we buy food to feed these people?" Jesus said this to test him, for he already knew what he was going to do.

Philip replied, "More than a half year's salary worth of food wouldn't be enough for each person to have even a little bit."

One of his disciples, Andrew, Simon Peter's brother, said, "A youth here has five barley loaves and two fish. But what good is that for a crowd like this?"

Jesus said, "Have the people sit down." There was plenty of grass there. They sat down, about five thousand of them. Then Jesus took the bread. When he had given thanks, he distributed it to those who were sitting there. He did the same with the fish, each getting as much as they wanted. When they had plenty to eat, he said to his disciples, "Gather up the leftover pieces, so that nothing will be wasted." So they gathered them and filled twelve baskets with the pieces of the five barley loaves that had been left over by those who had eaten.[21]

What are our expectations? Philip, one of Jesus's disciples is doing logistics. There is no way this is going to pencil out. If it were up to the disciples, everybody would stay hungry or go home. But Jesus sees the possibility and not the problem. There is a young boy who shares what little he has. Even though he probably knows there is no way his contribution is going to really change things, he still offers it in faith. Jesus takes what he gives and makes a miracle out of it. Lavish sharing invites lavish results. At the end of the day, everybody eats their fill and there are abundant leftovers. That's God's kingdom: abundant, overflowing, where everyone is cared for, and everybody has enough.

There is one detail in this story that always strikes me. Jesus's last instruction to his disciples is to gather up all the fragments so that nothing will be wasted or lost. That's the Jesus I've come to know. We see him throughout the gospels looking for the lost, the last, and the least. He is never satisfied until all the fragments—or better yet, the fragmented, the broken ones among us—are brought in, gathered up, and invited to the party. That is the Jesus who annoys the people who define their inclusion by the exclusion of others, the Pharisees of Jesus's time and ours. Why does Jesus eat with sinners and tax-collectors they ask? They are threatened by his new vision. They live by the rules of the old order.

The Final Confrontation

In the little town of Bethany, not far from Jerusalem, according to John's telling of the story, Jesus dines with his friends Mary, Martha, and their brother Lazarus, whom Jesus raised from the dead. The climax of the

---

21. John 6:5–13, CEB.

story comes when Mary takes a large amount of very expensive perfume and uses it to anoint Jesus's feet and then wipes them with her hair. The whole house is filled with the aroma of the perfume. Judas, the disciple who is about to betray Jesus, protests the reckless waste of resources and insists the perfume should have been sold and the money given to the poor. Jesus, however, sees Mary's lavish love and lets us know what is about to start happening in the story. "Leave her alone. This perfume was to be used in preparation for my burial, and this is how she used it. You will always have the poor among you, but you will not always have me"[22] Jesus, anointed by the Holy Spirit at his baptism for the work he was about to do is anointed again by this beloved woman. She alone perceives that Jesus's mission as the anointed, the messiah, will ultimately lead to his death and burial.[23] Indeed, the whole process is about to be set in motion.

We may remember the story of Jesus entering the city of Jerusalem on what we call Palm Sunday. I have stood on that same hillside, the Mount of Olives, and looked at Jerusalem. I have imagined what the day was like. I have imagined the people gathering palms and olive branches and escorting him into the city riding a donkey, coming as king. Did they know that what they were doing would be the first step in a journey leading to the young king's arrest, suffering, and death?

Jesus's act was a prophetic statement against the principalities and powers. As Jesus entered the city by the gates facing the Mount of Olives, it may very well have been the case that an alternative procession was happening across town emphasizing the might of Rome. During the festival of Passover, the Roman legion increased its presence, since this feast remembered how God had delivered the Jewish people out of slavery and led them to freedom in the Promised Land. The local Roman governor, Pontius Pilate, also made his way with the troops from his residence in

---

22. John 12:7–8, CEB.

23. A very similar story appears in Mark's Gospel on the Wednesday before Jesus's last supper. Mark adds a wonderful conclusion to Jesus's words about this act of devotion: "I tell you the truth that, wherever in the whole world the good news is announced, what she's done will also be told in memory of her" (Mark 14:9, CEB).

Caesarea-by-the-Sea into the city of Jerusalem to make his military presence known.

Imagine what a Roman military parade might have looked like—the sounds of armor moving through the narrow streets, weapons and horses on display, colorful banners and the golden eagles of Rome carried aloft, beating drums and even trumpets sounding, echoing off the walls. This procession not only demonstrated the might of Rome to keep public order, it was also a display of imperial theology. Caesar (in this case Emperor Tiberius) was not simply emperor, but the divine son of a god. His very real power over the lives of his subjects demonstrated his authority. Could the God of Israel say as much?

Jesus's procession also made use of symbols. The Mount of Olives was the place from which the prophets believed the great king of Israel would return to rule God's people. It was over the Mount of Olives that the presence of the Lord hovered briefly as it left the temple before the destruction of the city by the forces of Babylon. And that great returning king, according to the prophet Zechariah, would come back to Jerusalem riding on a donkey, but rather than a military victor, he would be a king of peace.[24]

In my congregation, we go into the streets on Palm Sunday proclaiming Jesus as the true Lord of the world and of our city of Los Angeles. We walk into our busy urban intersection with banners and bells and drums, a colorful and diverse parade of those who seek to follow the King of kings. We carry our Lord with us, present in the blessed sacrament of Holy Communion. As we re-enter the church, the choir leads us in the haunting words of a hymn:

> Ride on! ride on in majesty!
> In lowly pomp ride on to die;
> O Christ, thy triumphs now begin
> o'er captive death and conquered sin. . .
> Ride on! ride on in majesty!
> Thy last and fiercest strife is nigh;

---

24. See Borg and Crossan, *The Last Week*, 2–5, for a description of these competing processions..

the Father on his sapphire throne
expects his own anointed Son.
                    Ride on! ride on in majesty!
In lowly pomp ride on to die;
bow thy meek head to mortal pain,
then take, O God, thy power, and reign.[25]

Two processions entered the city of Jerusalem on that first Palm Sunday. The struggle was not so much about political protest as the great cosmic battle between the kingdoms of this world and the kingdom of God. Now the drama would unfold in the last week of Jesus's mortal life.

According to the gospels, one decisive event seems to be the tipping point over which the Jewish temple elites, who control the means of religious production, decide that Jesus must be dealt with. Jesus goes into the temple and performs an act of subversion. He overturns all the tables of those who change Roman currency for temple coinage. He disrupts the procurement of sacrificial animals, disrupting the whole temple economy and sacrificial system for a short time. Jesus offers a prophetic judgment in word and action. How could the God of Israel be aloof from God's people? How could God be controlled by means of the powerful and wealthy who claim a monopoly on getting right with God? The entire temple apparatus was corrupt and would soon come crashing down.

God's presence seen by Simeon and Ana in these very temple courts, present in the infant Jesus, was about to be made manifest by what Jesus was about to do in his confrontation with the powers and principalities of the world. All the grand collaboration with the powers of darkness would soon reach its ultimate end. Soon enough this very temple would be destroyed, but something new would emerge.

Thursday evening of that week was either the beginning of Passover, as we read the first three gospels, or the night before, if we read John. Regardless, the symbolic importance of this meal remains the same. Remember that on the night before they left Egypt, the Hebrews sacrificed a lamb and placed its blood on the doorpost as a sign that the angel of

---

25. Text by Henry Hart Milman, *The Hymnal 1982*.

death should "pass over" them. The book of Exodus tells the Jewish people to always remember this experience as if they themselves had been slaves in Egypt. At the Passover they would tell the story of God's covenant love for them, that God brought them out of slavery, led them through the wilderness into the new land of promise. On this night Jesus's disciples gather. Jesus seems to have known that all the wheels of intrigue were working. One of his own disciples, Judas collaborates with the temple authorities to set a trap for Jesus later that night.

During the meal, Jesus takes the unleavened Passover bread and says the traditional blessing over it. He breaks it and shares it, saying, "Take and eat; this is my body." In the same way he takes a cup of wine, says the blessing, and gives it to them, saying, "Drink this all of you, this is my blood of the covenant, which is poured out for many so that sins may be forgiven." Here again, Jesus calls us back to the book of Exodus where Moses ratifies the covenant with the blood of a lamb and sprinkles the people, saying, this is the blood of the covenant so that the sins of the people are forgiven.

Jesus predicts his own impending death and tells his closest friends that through his blood a new covenant will begin. Human sin needs no longer the sacrifice of lambs. One sacrifice will be offered to forgive the sins of many. Indeed, a new exodus is about to happen. From now on, all who share in this meal should consider themselves as having left bondage for freedom. Jesus the living way is going forward into this battle with darkness. In the Hebrew Bible, there is a story of Jesus's ancestor King David. As a young boy he fights a great warrior named Goliath on behalf of his people. Though he only has a slingshot, he conquers his mighty foe. Now Jesus, champion of his people, will stand in for them and win the victory like David did.

But John alone among the gospel writers describes a story of Jesus taking up a towel, bending down before his disciples, and washing their feet. Then he gets up and tells them he has given them an example, that they too should wash one another's feet. Jesus does for his disciples a similar thing as Mary did to him earlier in the week in Bethany, and he invites them to serve each other in this way. In John's story, Jesus will serve his disciples even more completely as he goes the next day to his own death. An early Christian hymn, later quoted by Paul in the letter to the Christians in the city of Philippi, reflects,

> Though he was in the form of God,
> he did not consider being equal with God something to exploit.
> But he emptied himself
> by taking the form of a slave
> and by becoming like human beings.
> When he found himself in the form of a human,
> he humbled himself by becoming obedient to the point of death,
> even death on a cross.[26]

The disciples and Jesus get up from the table and go out to the Garden of Gethsemane on the Mount of Olives. There Jesus will spend time in prayer, and even his three closest disciples, Peter, John, and James, won't be able to stay awake with him. He will experience a sense of unparalleled loneliness. And in this moment, the devil will find the opportune time to strike. I am sure Jesus met extreme fear and doubt knowing what would inevitably unfold in the coming hours. Is he totally mistaken about his identity, his mission? And yet, he can overcome all these doubts to accept his father's will.

What happens next is a whirlwind. Judas identifies Jesus as the rabbi they are looking for. The temple police come with torches and weapons and seize him. All his closest disciples flee in fear. The guards take Jesus back to the upper city of Jerusalem to the house of Caiaphas the high priest where Jesus receives a mock trial before the temple authorities. These are the people who hold authority because of their collusion with Roman economic and political power. These are the very people Jesus has spoken out against as betraying the true religion of Israel for their own gain. And these are the ones who will hand him over to the Roman governor, Pilate. Meanwhile, the gospels tell us Peter follows along at a distance and goes into the courtyard of Caiaphas's house only to deny Jesus not once,

---

26. Phil. 2:6–8, CEB.

but three times.[27] Early on Friday morning, they take Jesus to be interrogated by Pilate. After being cautioned by the Jerusalem authorities that to release Jesus, a would-be king, would be treason against Caesar, Pilate agrees to have him crucified, but before this, Jesus becomes the object of further humiliation.

In the city of Jerusalem today stands the Convent of the Sisters of Zion, built near what used to be the Antonia Fortress. It is probably not the place where Pilate interrogated Jesus and where the soldiers humiliated him. But in the pavement under the convent is an ancient stone used by Roman soldiers. It is a game board to play "the game of the king." They would take a prisoner they chose to especially humiliate and dress him in a robe with a fake crown and scepter. Then they would use sheep's-knuckle dice to decide who would get what meager possessions the prisoner had since he would no longer need them. During the game they would feign homage to him and beat him, further dehumanizing him before he would be led away to death, usually on a cross.

In our day, we see crosses on churches or as jewelry. In Jesus's day a cross was a sign of the most humiliating death possible. It was slow and agonizing, sometimes taking days before the victim would die. Crucifixions were usually done along some public road so that passersby would be cautioned not to let this happen to them. Crucifixion was the lot of terrorists or revolutionaries who dared to undermine the authority of Rome.

Outside the walls of Jerusalem was a hill in an old rock quarry called Skull Place where criminals were often crucified. After Jesus is humiliated and condemned, he is taken through the streets bearing the cross beam (not the full cross as we normally see depicted). He is crowned with the mock thorn crown, bloodied, beaten, and bruised, probably dazed and confused as he moves on outside the gates and up to Skull Place hill. There are vertical posts already planted in the ground. Jesus is stripped naked. Soldiers drive nails into his wrists and he's hoisted up so that the notch

---

27. I recommend reading the full accounts of Jesus's passion and death as they appear in each of the four Gospels. Each has a particular point of view from which they tell the story.

in the vertical beam receives the cross beam where his hands have been nailed. Then his feet are nailed to the vertical post.

As Jesus struggles to breathe he has what may be his final temptation: to despair, to think all this has been in vain. He cries out the in words of the psalmist, "My God, my God, why have you forsaken me?" The gospels differ on the words Jesus speaks from the cross, but clearly, we can imagine his near panic at this moment. Also, I can imagine Jesus comes to a reawakened knowledge of the work he is doing.

Luke tells us a criminal crucified next to Jesus calls out, "Jesus, remember me when you come into your kingdom." Jesus tells him, "Today you will be with me in paradise." The one who leads the way forward receives another disciple, not by the Sea of Galilee, but in these final moments into the future.[28] Luke gives Jesus's last words as "Father, into your hands I commend my Spirit"; again he quotes the Psalms, but we see a resolve, an understanding that he has done what he has been given to do. And yet even here, he knows only that he has been faithful. It is his Father who will transform what he has done. He dies in faith that the future will be in God's hands.

Jesus's faithful disciples, primarily the women who stayed with him at the cross, see to his body. We are told there is a rock tomb nearby, a common place of burial in ancient Judea. It belongs to a wealthy man named Joseph from the town of Arimathea, who was a follower of Jesus. He wraps the body of Jesus in a clean linen shroud. There is no time for all the typical rites of anointing and wrapping the body. The afternoon is getting late and the Passover Sabbath will soon begin, so they hurry about their work. They may have left Jesus's body on a slab in the tomb until they could come back and finish the preparations. A stone is rolled over the entrance. They go away. A sword of sorrow has indeed pierced the heart of his mother, who treasures her son in her heart. Mary Magdalene and the other faithful women begin the Sabbath rest grieving and inconsolable.

I stand before an altar depicting the scene of the crucifixion. Below it are outcroppings of rock from an ancient quarry. I kneel and bow low to

---

28. See Luke 23:41–43.

place my hand in the cleft of one of these rocks. Here in this very place, tradition tells us, is the Skull Place—Calvary—where Jesus was crucified. Down below in a small chapel is a rock cleft by an earthquake; here a legend says Adam was buried and as the blood of Jesus poured from the cross onto the ground, it flowed down this crevice onto the grave of Adam. This story is not historical, but it is true. Adam, representing all of us who wander far away, is brought near again by means of the God who came among us in the flesh, Jesus. The blood of the covenant joins all of us into one blood, one new family.

Today, the place of Jesus's death and burial is covered by a single enormous church. Near the place of the tomb is the anointing stone, the place tradition says Jesus's body was anointed and wrapped in a shroud before being placed in the tomb. For generations people have come here from all over the world to kneel and pray. They may anoint a special cross or cloth. Sometimes they bring shrouds with which they will bury a loved one. I kneel with other pilgrims and touch my forehead to the marble slab, and then kiss it. I have not brought anything with me, but I take off my scarf and rub it on the stone as others also do. I place it again around my neck, thinking how similar this is—almost identical—to a practice in my own church community halfway around the world:

On Maundy or Holy Thursday night, we begin what we call the Great Three Days, remembering Jesus's last supper, his death and burial, and, finally, the Resurrection. At the end of Thursday evening, it is our practice to strip the altar of all decoration—altar cloths, candles, etc. The altar traditionally has been a symbol of Christ, so symbolically we see Jesus stripped of his garments, left alone in his journey to the cross to battle the dark lord. We also wash and anoint the altar with water and scented holy oil called chrism. In fact, the scent of the chrism fills the whole cathedral. Then members of our community come forward to dry the altar. We never have to ask twice to have people participate in this ritual. Even strangers who have never been to our congregation before naturally come forward and tenderly dry the altar table. It was exactly the same image I saw at the anointing stone, people kneeling down, wiping the stone with their scarves or cloths.

On the next day, Good Friday, a similar event takes place. We carry a large embroidered cloth icon of Jesus lying in the tomb and place it in the midst of the congregation. We have flowers for people and we invite them all to come and reverence the icon. Some people stand, but many kneel and place their foreheads on the icon in prayer; some kiss it, No one rushes, but they stay with this moment. I do, too. As I look at the image of Jesus, battered, crucified, dead, I'm reminded of a line from a hymn: "By his tomb, Christ makes room." I remember all those who have gone before me whom I have loved and lost. I'm sure that is what others are doing. And more, I think that this is the place to which I will one day come. So will you. It is our shared human condition. Make room for me, I pray. Jesus, remember me when you come into your kingdom.

But this moment cannot be all. If that's all there is, why do we come here to venerate a long-dead prophet, no matter how inspiring his message? This is a scene, but it's not the whole drama. I think again of those faithful disciples tenderly placing the body of Jesus on the cold stone, sealing the tomb, and walking away as the Sabbath was about to arrive. The words of the poet Jane Kenyon, who died too young, come rushing to my mind:

Let the light of late afternoon
shine through chinks in the barn, moving
up the bales as the sun moves down.

Let the cricket take up chafing
as a woman takes up her needles
and her yarn. Let evening come.

Let dew collect on the hoe abandoned
in long grass. Let the stars appear
and the moon disclose her silver horn.

Let the fox go back to its sandy den.
Let the wind die down. Let the shed
go black inside. Let evening come.

To the bottle in the ditch, to the scoop
in the oats, to air in the lung

let evening come.
    Let it come, as it will, and don't
be afraid. God does not leave us
comfortless, so let evening come.[29]

Questions for Reflection

1. When you hear the word "repent," what does it bring up for you? What does Jesus mean by this word in the Gospels?
2. In the Gospel of John, the first words Jesus speaks are these: "What are you looking for?" Imagine Jesus saying those words to you. How do you answer?
3. The parables portray a world that seems to be very different from the one we take for granted. What do you think about a God who pays everyone the same even when they do less work, or more? What about a God who accepts the prodigal back with a lavish party? What do these stories tell us about God? What do they say about us?
4. How does Jesus's story provide us a way, a path, a map for our lives?
5. What is most challenging about the way of Jesus for you?
6. How do you understand the impact of Jesus's final confrontation with the powers of darkness for your life?
7. Read again Jane Kenyon's poem "Let Evening Come." What images stand out for you? How does this poem reflect on our human mortality in which Jesus shared?

---

29. "Let Evening Come" by Jane Kenyon. Copyright 2005 by The Estate of Jane Kenyon. Reprinted with permission of The Permission Company, Inc. on behalf of Graywolf Press, Minneapolis MN, www.graywolfpress.org.

6

Jesus—The Truth and the Life

Very truly, I tell you, you will weep and mourn, but the world will rejoice; you will have pain, but your pain will turn into joy. When a woman is in labor, she has pain, because her hour has come. But when her child is born, she no longer remembers the anguish because of the joy of having brought a human being into the world. So you have pain now; but I will see you again, and your hearts will rejoice, and no one will take your joy from you."[1]

Jesus died. Most of his disciples scattered in disbelief, grief, and disillusionment. His body was removed from the cross, hurriedly wrapped in spices and linen, and buried. The tomb was sealed. Jesus's disciples rested and waited during the Sabbath. Yet each gospel writer continues the story, although the details vary. Here is Mark's version:

---

1. John 16:20–22.

When the Sabbath was over, Mary Magdalene, Mary the mother of James, and Salome bought spices so that they could go and anoint Jesus' dead body. Very early on the first day of the week, just after sunrise, they came to the tomb. They were saying to each other, "Who's going to roll the stone away from the entrance for us?" When they looked up, they saw that the stone had been rolled away. (And it was a very large stone!) Going into the tomb, they saw a young man in a white robe seated on the right side; and they were startled. But he said to them, "Don't be alarmed! You are looking for Jesus of Nazareth, who was crucified. He has been raised. He isn't here. Look, here's the place where they laid him. Go, tell his disciples, especially Peter, that he is going ahead of you into Galilee. You will see him there, just as he told you." Overcome with terror and dread, they fled from the tomb. They said nothing to anyone, because they were afraid.[2]

Mark's terse style and sense of urgency highlights the strangeness of the situation. Women come to the tomb after the Sabbath to complete the burial ritual. The heavy stone is already rolled away and they encounter this strange young man. We can call him an angel since he bears a message of good news. Jesus isn't here. He is risen. Go and tell his disciples. It's these witnesses—women—who are to be the first apostles. They are the ones who have the privilege of sharing this good news. And yet the news is so unbelievable, disconcerting, terrifying, that I imagine them dropping their burial ointments and getting out of there as quick as they can "because they were afraid." That's how Mark leaves it.

Do you find it strange that this is the end of the Gospel? Other people did, too. They wanted to tell the rest of the story, make the conclusion tidier. So, there are two additional endings pinned on to Mark, but we are pretty sure that the original ended in just this way.

Why might Mark have done this? Some scholars think that because his gospel was written in a time of persecution, the ending we have was

---

2. Mark 16:1–8, CEB.

all he was able to complete before he either had to flee or was arrested. Others say the original ending is lost to history. Still others suggest he had a reason for this ending. I agree with the latter, and think it was twofold. First, this gospel would have originally been read aloud in the midst of the gathered community of believers or seekers. Mark's audience would have asked, as we do, "What happened next?" Since you and I are reading the same text two thousand years later, something else must have happened. Those women overcame their fear and were moved with enough faith to tell somebody else—Jesus's disciples, and maybe others as well, about what they had seen and heard. You and I, who have also heard this story from these women, need also to move from fear to faith and tell others about the experience of resurrection.

What else does the young man in white tell the women? "Jesus is going ahead of you into Galilee. There you will see him." This is the second clue to the mystery Mark wants to unfold. What if Mark is saying that Jesus is going ahead of *us* into Galilee? How will we recognize him? Remember, Mark begins in Galilee. Mark invites us to start reading the Gospel again, this time with resurrection eyes. If we go back to Galilee, where the story begins, there will we see Jesus: he is risen and present right now and he speaks to us out of the pages of the Gospel. Hear him speak to you. Remember the first words he says: "Now is the time! Here comes God's kingdom! Change your hearts and lives (repent) and trust this good news." Remember that "repent" means to turn around and take another direction, to open your heart to a new possibility. That's what Mark wants us to do—open our hearts to the possibility of resurrection, of new life, that the kingdom of God has begun. Trust that the good news really is that good.

What Really Happened?

Like those first hearers, we want to ask whether this really happened. Did Jesus really rise from the dead, or is there some other explanation? Sceptics in every age, including those in the first century, came up with alternative explanations: his body was stolen, or he didn't really die. He was still alive when they took him down from the cross and his disciples nursed him back to health. If any of these alternatives were true, why would his disciples have gone to their deaths proclaiming their belief in the Resurrection, and wouldn't someone have debunked the whole thing with hard evidence?

Especially in our post-Enlightenment age, revisionists have attempted to explain the rise of Christianity by means other than the reality of the Resurrection. One explanation is cognitive dissonance, in which people want something so badly to be true that they continue strongly to proclaim it even in the face of contrary evidence. The disciples weren't expecting Jesus to be risen from the dead. It was a shocking surprise. By all accounts, the disciples spent that first Sabbath after Jesus's death thinking they had followed a failed messiah like so many others before him and indeed after.[3]

Recently, I heard a speaker say that he thought the Resurrection was a strong spiritual vision in which the disciples saw Jesus appear to them in a dream and this experience was so powerful and comforting that they were fortified in the belief that Jesus was still with them. He noted that people often have profound dream experiences where the dead seem to visit them and these experiences are very real for them. The disciples' experience was not that different, he argued.

I understand what he is saying about dreams. I had a similar experience several years ago. One of my closest friends, Matthew, died at the age of twenty-five from complications due to AIDS. I missed him terribly and couldn't accept that he was no longer alive. One night I was in a state of half-sleep and had a clear sense of Matthew coming into my room, leaning over me, taking my hand and saying, "I love you, but it's time for me to go. Please let me go now." It was very real. It was profound. It helped move me through my process of grief, but it was not a resurrection. People in Jesus's day had similar experiences. In fact, reports of being visited by "ghosts" or spirits were quite common. The Gospels and the rest of the New Testament are quite clear that this experience was unique.

---

3. Wright, *Surprised by Hope*, 60.

The Gospels say that the tomb was empty and that Jesus himself in a physical way met his disciples after the Resurrection. Both of these things point to the historical reality of the Resurrection of Jesus in the flesh. The Jesus of Easter was not just a resuscitated Jesus; he was different. The Gospels tell us the disciples didn't recognize him at first. Yet, he was, in fact, the Jesus they had followed and continued to follow after Easter morning.

The history-changing nature of Jesus's death and resurrection means that a whole new order of creation began early on a Sunday morning before the sun had risen. As Bishop Tom Wright says:

> The resurrection of Jesus offers itself . . . not as an absurd event within the old world but the symbol and starting point of the new world. The claim advanced by Christianity is of that magnitude: Jesus of Nazareth ushers in not simply a new religious possibility, not simply a new ethic or a new way of salvation, but a new creation.[4]

The old order, especially the post-Enlightenment world in which we live, cannot accept its reality-defining claims to be challenged by a new creation breaking into the present. The old order says:, "We know how the world works and resurrection is impossible. Therefore, it could not have happened." More than that, the old order says, "We know how the political and economic order works. The rules of the kingdom of God, of the New Creation are foolish according to the harsh realities of the world as we know it. We oppose anything that does not play by our rules of the game."

On the contrary, what Christians traditionally have said and continue to say, despite claims of revisionists, is that we can make a historical claim about the reality of the Resurrection, even as that reality transcends our ability to know it empirically. If the message of Easter is true, it continues to be available to you and me. We can begin reading the Gospel of Mark and meet the Jesus who goes ahead of us into Galilee. New Testament scholar Luke Timothy Johnson puts it this way:

---

4. Wright, *Surprised by Hope*, 67.

The "Easter visions [of the first disciples] give narrative expression to an experience that far transcended the encounters of select individuals. The resurrection experience that founded and that grounds the church is not based on the transitory encounters of a few people on Easter day or for forty days thereafter, but on the experience of power through Jesus by generations of people across the centuries and continuing until today.[5]

So the risen Jesus is not a figure of the past available to us through the archeology of places or texts, or one who can be dug up or unmasked with enough clever academic sleuthing or narrative skill. Rather, Jesus is a living Lord available to us today through the Holy Spirit who continues to work in the lives of believers and of the church. (More on the Holy Spirit later.)

Let's explore some of the other stories of the Resurrection with this in mind: the Gospel writers don't simply present something that happened long ago and far away, but someone whom we can encounter through them. Let's also remember that these stories and the other New Testament reflections on Jesus's Resurrection cannot be easily described and so we are moved to poetry, song, and narrative to understand what happened and what continues to happen as the risen Jesus meets us in our world today.

Meeting Jesus in Three Easter Stories

Each of the Gospels presents the same basic outline of the events of Easter morning. Early on Sunday, the first day of the week, the faithful women who followed Jesus come to the tomb and the stone is rolled away. In John, there is only one woman reported, Mary Magdalene. Every gospel mentions her among those who go to the tomb. Jesus is not there; the tomb is empty. There is an encounter with mysterious messengers.

---

5. Johnson, *The Real Jesus*,135. Johnson gives an excellent summary and critique of the revisionist project to unearth a historical Jesus unmoored from the Jesus of Christian faith, as seen for example in projects such as the Jesus Seminar.

In all but John's Gospel the messengers proclaim to the women that Jesus is risen from the dead. John tells a different and wonderful story about Mary Magdalene's experience. Apart from these central details, the Gospels differ as to who was present, what the mysterious messengers said, and what happened when the women got there. The stories about the appearances of Jesus to his followers after this first event differ as well. We won't look at all of them. We will explore a few of the stories to help us see the message the early church sought to give us about the Resurrection and to outline a picture of the risen Lord for our own lives.

Walking to Emmaus (Luke 24:13–35)

Luke tells us that on the evening of Easter Day two disciples are walking along the road outside of Jerusalem dazed, confused, and dejected. They had high hopes that Jesus would be the Messiah, but their hopes had been dashed. They try to come to grips with the story the women told about the tomb being open. Jesus was no longer there and angels said he was alive. As they walk along, a mysterious stranger joins them on their journey. He asks what they are talking about and they tell their tale. The stranger then begins to open up the Scriptures to them, to explain how the prophets said that the Messiah would indeed suffer and come into his glory.

Finally, they get to the village of Emmaus. Since it is getting dark, they invite him to stay with them. They sit down to share a meal and the stranger takes the bread, blesses it, and breaks it; suddenly, they realize that they have been with Jesus the whole time. As soon as they recognize him, he vanishes from their sight. The disciples turn to one another and agree that their hearts were on fire as he opened the Scriptures and they gained new insight about the Messiah's mission. Jesus really was the one they were looking for. They get up and rush back to Jerusalem to tell the other disciples of their experience with the risen Lord.

While there is a lot we could say about this story, a few things are central. First, Jesus meets the disciples where they are, both physically and also in their state of confusion and dejection. He gives them insight into their experience. He turns them around—opens their hearts to see a new hope and possibility even in the midst of their sadness and grief. Luke brings us this story so we too can know that the Risen One is with us on our journey even when we're in the dark. Through prayer and reflection, through being with one another, we can meet him and find hope and direction for our lives.

Second, notice that the disciples had a taken-for-granted understanding about what the Scriptures said about the Messiah. When they experience the risen Jesus, they gain new insight into what the Scriptures mean. We will talk about this later, but for now notice that the experience of Resurrection gives us new eyes to see the story of God's plan for us and for the whole world.

Third, when Luke describes feeding the multitude, earlier in his gospel, Jesus takes the loaves of bread, he looks up to heaven, blesses and breaks them, and gives them to the disciples. Jesus uses the same pattern—taking, blessing, breaking, and giving—at the Last Supper and asks them to continue to do this in remembrance of him. When Jesus does this same action at Emmaus, they remember what he did and recognize him.

Yet Jesus eludes us. That is a common description in almost all the gospel stories of the risen Jesus. He is present, his disciples experience him, and then he is gone. It's as if we can't hold on to Jesus. He is always going on ahead of us, leading us forward into our future. This last insight gives us a sense of how the risen Lord breaks into our world from the new creation. Time and space aren't absolute constructs. They are permeable. There's another world that's both present and absent. That new world becomes clearer in perhaps one of the most beautiful stories in the Bible, John's tale of Mary Magdalene on Easter morning.

Why Do You Weep? (John 20:11–18)

Mary Magdalene is the first to discover the empty tomb in John's Gospel, but she immediately runs and brings Peter and John who sees and believes; at least, he believes the tomb is empty. Does he or Peter know any more than that? They go back to where they are staying. Mary doesn't leave; she stays in the garden looking into the darkness of the grave.

Let's go backwards in the story to the night Jesus was arrested. John tells us that after Jesus and his disciples leave the table at the last supper, they go out to a garden across the Kidron Valley. Judas, the betrayer, knows where to find Jesus. He and a group of soldiers go to the garden. When they come upon Jesus and the disciples, Peter takes out a sword and tries to defend Jesus. He cuts off the ear of the high priest's slave, Malchus. Jesus tells Peter to put away the sword. Then they arrest and bind Jesus. Think back to the second chapter of this book, or better, the second and third chapters of Genesis. That story takes place in a garden: Eden. The serpent is there to do his work. He entices Eve and Adam to plot against God. So here, the old serpent, the devil, is at work plotting against God's mission of saving humankind in this garden across the Kidron Valley. The power struggle of the old creation is playing out.

There is another garden outside the city of Jerusalem and we hear about it after the powers of hell have done their worst and Jesus has died on the cross. John tells us that Joseph of Arimathea and another disciple, Nicodemus, come to take the body of Jesus from the cross. Nicodemus provides about a hundred pounds of myrrh and aloes, fragrant burial spices. They wrap the body in the spices and linen and lay Jesus in a tomb in the garden. The stench of death must have been overwhelmed by the odor of all that perfume. John may remember this detail because it reminds him of the epic love poem from the Hebrew Scriptures, the Song of Solomon:[6]

> How sweet is your love, my sister, my bride!
> How much better is your love than wine,
> and the fragrance of your oils than any spice! . . .
> myrrh and aloes,
> with all chief spices—
> a garden fountain, a well of living water, and flowing streams from
>   Lebanon.

---

6. See Griffith-Jones, *The Four Witnesses*, 400–404, for the full reflection on the connection between the Song of Solomon and this poignant story in John's Gospel.

Awake, O north wind,
And come, O south wind!
Blow upon my garden
That its fragrance may be wafted abroad.
Let my beloved come to his garden
And eat its choicest fruit.
I come to my garden, my sister, my bride;
I gather my myrrh with my spice. . .[7]

This part of the story closes with dramatic irony: the scent of perfume in place of decay, springtime in the midst of winter, a remembered love song in the face of violence and hate, a garden in the place of death.

On the first day of the week, as the sun is rising, Mary Magdalene remains in this garden. Her tears obscure her vision. The smell of myrrh and spices is still heavy in the air from the open grave. She peers inside the darkness and meets two angels all in white, one at the head of the resting place of Jesus and one at the feet. They ask, "Why are you weeping?"—

"They have taken away my Lord and I do not know where they have laid him." She turns around and sees a stranger who she thinks may be the gardener.

He, too, asks, "Woman, why do you weep? Whom do you seek?" Disoriented, she asks him where he has taken Jesus so she can carry him away. Then the stranger calls her name, "Mary." John tells us she turns and recognizes him.

"Rabbouni!" she calls, an Aramaic word of endearment for a beloved teacher. She seems to want to embrace him, but he says, "Don't hold on to me, because I've not gone to the father, but go tell my brothers I am ascending to my Father and your Father, to my God and your God."

Mary leaves the garden not in fear, but absolute joy to tell the other disciples, "I have seen the Lord!"

This garden also recalls Eden, but this time there is no serpent. Instead, there is the strange gardener who goes unrecognized until he calls the name of the woman. Mary. In that first garden, God calls out,

---

7. Song of Sol. 4:10, 14b–15:1a.

looking for Adam and Eve, "Where are you?" In this garden, Jesus finds the one he seeks and calls her name. Unlike the woman in Eden, Mary doesn't hide herself from God the gardener, but turns, and turns again. I'm reminded of the well-known Shaker song "Simple Gifts:"

> And when we find ourselves in the place just right,
> 'Twill be in the valley of love and delight.
> To turn, turn will be our delight,
> Till by turning, turning we come 'round right.

The Shakers call this a dancing song and the words "turn, turn" are directions for the choreography. I imagine Mary in the joyful dance of turning, turning as she meets the gardener. The Sabbath rest has ended and a whole new creation has begun on this Easter Day. The work of the serpent has been crushed and Mary has opened her heart to believe in a whole new possibility.

And yet, she first misunderstands. Mary thinks her Rabbouni has returned to her for the same old relationship they shared. But she will not be the bride imagined in the Song of Solomon, or at least not only her. The bride will be the whole new community of love that begins on this morning; she cannot hold on to him. He will no longer be held back by the constraints of his physical presence among his disciples. Mary has seen the Lord, and so will others on that Easter Day.

You and I and millions of others can meet the Risen One with the sure and certain hope of God's new creation starting right now, and continuing into eternity. The burial service in the Episcopal Book of Common Prayer announces this hope in words from the nineteenth chapter of the book of Job:

> "As for me, I know that my redeemer lives
> And that at the last he will stand upon the earth.
> After my awaking, he will raise me up and in my body I shall see
>   God.
> I myself shall see, and my eyes behold him
> Who is my friend and not a stranger."[8]

---

8. The Book of Common Prayer, 1979, 491.

Like the first disciples on the road to Emmaus, we can look back at the rich stories of the Hebrew Bible and gain new insight because of the Jesus experience. We can also look forward, not just to what happens when we pass through the veil of this life, but also when the fullness of the new creation comes and God transforms the old world into the new. A poet named simply Aisling writes, "And when the last sun fails to rise I shall wake to find you in the garden with my name on your lips."[9]

Believe (John 20:19–29)

John continues his story on Easter night. The disciples are locked behind closed doors, afraid that the powers that came after Jesus are coming for them. Suddenly, Jesus appears with them and says, "Peace be with you." He shows them his wounded hands and feet and they are filled with joy. Again, he says, "Peace be with you; as the father sent me, so I'm sending you." Then he breathes on them and says, "Receive the Holy Spirit. Whoever you forgive will be forgiven, if you don't forgive them, they aren't forgiven."

Again, we are reminded of the creation story. Like the Spirit who blew over the face of the waters at the dawn of time, Jesus breathes his Spirit over the new community he is forming in the world. It is a new community of citizens of another country—a new community of love, peace, and forgiveness continuing the work of the Risen One in the world. He has a material presence that continues his earthly existence. He bears the marks of his suffering and death, but there is something different about him. Like the story of Emmaus and the story of Mary Magdalene, his close friends don't recognize him at first. What's more, he transcends the confines of space and time. He can be with them behind locked doors.

We hear that Thomas, one of Jesus's chosen twelve disciples, is not there to see the risen Lord. He is skeptical of what his friends have told him. He will not believe unless he conducts an experiment. He has to probe

---

9. Aisling, "To Jesus on Holy Saturday."

the wounds and verify that it is Jesus before he will believe their story. The next Sunday evening they are all gathered and the doors are locked. Sure enough, Jesus stands in the midst of them and offers the same greeting, "Peace be with you." Then he goes directly to Thomas and places himself under his gaze. "Touch my hands, see the wounds, place your hand on my side, see where they thrust the spear after I died. Verify that I am not a ghost, or a vision. I'm flesh and blood—stop doubting. Believe."

At this point, Thomas opens his heart to the new possibility. The story doesn't tell us he needs the physical verification, although artists like Caravaggio have created extraordinary paintings depicting Thomas as the probing investigator, the scientist we might say, needing material evidence to make a conclusion. In the end, Thomas leaves that behind. He simply confesses, "My Lord and my God."

Jesus says, "Do you believe because you see me? Blessed are those who have not seen and yet believe." Jesus turns to us and says, in effect, "blessed are *you*" Blessed are those who would like to verify, dig into things, see for themselves, and yet at some point open their hearts to a new possibility beyond material evidence. We have not had the experience of Thomas. We have not had the experience of those first disciples, and yet we are invited to open our hearts to the possibility of new life, of resurrection, of Jesus in our midst. The Risen One stands before us and asks us whether we will leave behind our need for scientific verification of ineffable truths, will we step into a new world, a new way of knowing; will we too believe?

Morning Has Broken on a Whole New Creation

The meeting of Jesus and Mary Magdalene is all about a new Garden, a new Eden. Remember that Jesus tells Mary he must ascend to his father. I think we can sometimes misunderstand the meaning of Jesus's words, especially if we are familiar with the story of the ascension of Jesus as Luke tells it. Jesus and the disciples go to the town of Bethany outside Jerusalem and while he blesses them he "withdraws" from them and is carried up into heaven. The language makes us think that heaven is a place "up there" somewhere. Illuminations in medieval manuscripts and paintings by other artists have made the image concrete and almost comical, with the disciples gazing up at Jesus while only his feet dangle above them inside of the frame of the image.

When I was a brash undergraduate student I asked my medieval philosophy professor, "I'm supposed to believe that a first-century Jewish man from the Middle East is floating someplace up in the heavens so that it could theoretically be possible to actually find him physically?" My patient professor informed me that I was being too materialist in my thinking. He explained the concept of dimensionality the ancient writers were attempting to convey to my all-too-literal undergraduate self: that the risen Jesus passed into another dimension—a future dimension we might call it—heaven, the kingdom of God or the New Creation. In Jesus's resurrection, that heavenly reality entered into our world. Now the old order overlaps with the new one. This may seem a bit difficult to grasp. That's why Paul, one of the early Christian writers of the New Testament, explains it in his letter to the Christians in Rome:

> We know that the whole creation is groaning together and suffering labor pains up until now. And it's not only the creation. We ourselves who have the Spirit as the first crop of the harvest also groan inside as we wait to be adopted and for our bodies to be set free. We were saved in hope. If we see what we hope for, that isn't hope. Who hopes for what they already see? But if we hope for what we don't see, we wait for it with patience.[10]

When Paul talks about the new creation he means several things. First, it has already begun in the death and resurrection of Jesus. When Jesus died he served as our champion, fighting all the powers of death and evil that had enslaved us. Remember when the people of Israel were slaves under Pharaoh? The New Testament uses that imagery to describe humankind enslaved to the powers of the world that seek to turn us away from God's hope for us. Jesus rescued us and opens the door into God's new dimension of life.

---

10. Rom. 8:22–25, CEB.

Remember how John makes much of Jesus's mistaken identity as the gardener in the story we discussed earlier? Who was given the vocation to be gardener in Eden? Adam. John wants us to see Jesus the gardener as a sort of representative new Adam. Paul also takes up the analogy of Jesus as the new Adam. In his first letter to the church in Corinth, Paul says, "Christ has been raised from the dead. He's the first crop of the harvest of those who have died. Since death came through a human being, the resurrection of the dead came through one too. In the same way that everyone dies in Adam, so also everyone will be given life in Christ."[11]

Second, the new creation continues to be born in the world in each person who joins with Jesus to be part of it and shares that same vision. Remember when Jesus breathes on his first disciples and says receive the Holy Spirit? We too receive that same Spirit in our baptism—the presence of God living within us. Because of this, we become part of the new creation reclaimed by God from the powers of this world that work against God's purposes. We are "adopted" as God's children, restored to our rightful relationship with God.

Jesus is talking about this sort of relationship when he tells the story of the son who wandered far away from his father. We human beings are like that, wanting a relationship with our creator, but not knowing how to do it. We may think we can only be slaves of God, doing all sorts of things to get back into God's good graces, but that's not the answer. The good news is that when we come to God through our relationship with Jesus we are welcomed back home.

Third, the whole created order is waiting for the new creation to emerge in its fullness. That includes the earth and all her creatures. When I hear again Eleanor Farjeon's beautiful old hymn "Morning Has Broken," I think about that hope for the restoration of all creation as God intended in Eden:

Morning has broken like the first morning,
Blackbird has spoken like the first bird;
Praise for the singing, praise for the morning,
Praise for them springing fresh from the Word.

---

11. I Cor. 15:20–22, CEB.

Sweet the rain's new fall sunlit from heaven,
Like the first dewfall on the first grass;
Praise for the sweetness of the wet garden,
Sprung in completeness where His feet pass.

Mine is the sunlight, mine is the morning,
Born of the one light Eden saw play;
Praise with elation, praise every morning,
God's re-creation of the new day.

When I go out in my back garden as the sun rises and I see hummingbirds taking a drink from the fountain, hear doves waking up and cooing, and the neighbors' chickens exulting, I can experience the simple beauty of creation. But I know it isn't Eden. I know what we humans have done to the world. I know about environmental degradation. I know about wars and violence. I know that many people do not wake up to experience the beauty of nature. That's why this hymn gives us hope for God's re-creation of the new day. As C. S Lewis observes:

At present we are on the outside of the world, the wrong side of the door. We discern the freshness and purity of morning, but they do not make us fresh and pure. We cannot mingle with the splendors we see. But all the leaves of the New Testament are rustling with the rumor that it will not always be so. Some day, God willing, we shall get in.[12]

So the loveliness we see in this creation reflects a future beauty one day to be revealed. The works of human creativity I savor, the acts of love, justice, and care for the earth in which I and others engage, are wonderful signs of the future in the present, but they are not the fullness of the new creation. We aren't there yet. We glimpse the future and "some day, God willing, we shall get in."

---

12. Lewis, *The Weight of Glory*, 43.

Paul envisions the new creation to be about tearing down barriers between people—especially the barriers between the rest of humankind and the Jewish people whose vocation was to direct humanity back home. In his letter to the Christians in the Roman province of Galatia (in modern Turkey), Paul tells the Gentile Christians, "Being circumcised or not being circumcised doesn't mean anything. What matters is a new creation"[13] In one of his letters to the Corinthian Christians, Paul says, "If anyone is in Christ, that person is part of the new creation. The old things have gone away, and look, new things have arrived"[14] In other words, it used to be the case that circumcision and the Jewish law were the only markers that demonstrated a restored relationship with God. Now, God has become one of us in Jesus and points the way to the divine celebration. Everyone is invited, no matter who we are. To be "in Christ" means to be claimed by him in baptism and marked as his own forever so that nothing can ever separate you from God's love.

Through the Veil

When Jesus dies, Mark, Luke, and Matthew add a strange detail. They tell us the curtain in the temple was torn in two. If we had been in the temple in Jerusalem and we entered into the place where the priests offered sacrifice and then we went further into the holy place, we would have seen a curtain—actually a richly embroidered tapestry. Josephus, an ancient Jewish historian tells us it was deep blue and embroidered in purple and scarlet and the constellations of the stars were emblazoned all across it so that when you looked at it, you saw an image of all the heavens before you. On the other side of the curtain was the "Holy of Holies." In chapter 4, we described how the high priest would enter to offer sacrifice on behalf of all the people once a year, on the Day of Reconciliation or Atonement.

---

13. Gal. 6:15, CEB.
14. 2 Cor. 5:17, CEB.

The Gospel writers want us to understand that in Jesus's death, and subsequently through his resurrection and ascension, Jesus entered into the heavenly Holy of Holies as a high priest. The wall of separation keeping us out of Eden was now broken down and instead of sacrifices needing to be offered again and again to make us right with God, God in the flesh offered himself as the last sacrifice; no other one would be needed again. The author of the Letter to the Hebrews reflects on the temple analogy:

> Christ didn't enter the holy place (which is a copy of the true holy place) made by human hands, but into heaven itself, so that he now appears in God's presence for us. He didn't enter to offer himself over and over again, like the high priest enters the earthly holy place every year with blood that isn't his. If that were so, then Jesus would have to suffer many times since the foundation of the world. Instead, he has now appeared once at the end of the ages to get rid of sin by sacrificing himself. People are destined to die once and then face judgment. In the same way, Christ was also offered once to take on himself the sins of many people. He will appear a second time, not to take away sin but to save those who are eagerly waiting for him.[15]

Jesus took on our human flesh in every way except sin, and now takes our human nature right into the very presence of God. God's presence also comes to us through the Holy Spirit who dwells in our hearts. God's grace, mercy, and love are ours if we will allow ourselves to enter into that relationship. The Letter to the Hebrews tells us that Jesus is our "Pioneer" who has gone before us into God's presence. He is also our "Perfecter," transforming us into God's vision of who God created you and me to be and to become.[16] There will be a day when the new creation will be a reality on earth as it is in heaven. Jesus who entered the heavenly temple

---

15. Heb. 9:24–28, CEB.
16. Heb. 12:2.

will transform the whole cosmos into a temple—that's what God intended from the very beginning.

In my congregation, at the Great Vigil of Easter, after we celebrate baptism there is a moment of silence, we then proclaim part of an Easter sermon written in the fourth century by one of the early bishops of the Christian church, John Chrysostom:

> If any be lovers of God, let them rejoice in this beautiful and radiant feast.
>
> Enter all of you, into the joy of your master.
>
> First and last, receive alike your reward. Rich and poor, dance together.
>
> Come, all of you, share in the banquet of faith: draw on the wealth of God's mercy.
>
> Let no one lament their poverty; for the universal kingdom has been revealed.
>
> Let no one weep for their sins; for the light of forgiveness has risen from the grave.
>
> Let no one fear death; for the death of the Savior has set us free.
>
> He has destroyed death by undergoing death.
>
> He has despoiled hell by descending into hell.
>
> O death, where is your sting? O hell, where is your victory?
>
> Christ is risen, and you are cast down. Christ is risen, and demons are fallen.
>
> Christ is risen, and the angels rejoice. Christ is risen, and life reigns in freedom.
>
> Christ is risen, and the grave is emptied of the dead.

Then the reader calls out "Alleluia! Christ is risen." We all shout in reply, "The Lord is risen indeed. Alleluia!" Bells ring, people beat drums, and we start singing, "Christ is risen from the dead, trampling down death by death, and on those in the tombs bestowing life." Some start to dance, turning and turning. We are in the garden and we hear his voice, each of our names on his lips.

Questions for Reflection

1. Bishop Tom Wright says, "Jesus of Nazareth ushers in not simply a new religious possibility, not simply a new ethic or a new way of salvation, but a new creation." If this is true, then Easter changes everything for us. How do you understand Jesus's resurrection? What implications does the resurrection have for our lives or for the whole world?

2. What Easter story discussed in this chapter most resonates with you? Why?

3. How can we experience the presence of the risen Jesus in our lives and communities today?

7

Believing

Now Jesus did many other signs in the presence of his disciples,
which are not written in this book. But these are written so that
you may come to believe that Jesus is the Messiah, the Son of
God, and that through believing you may have life in his name.
—John 20:30–31

During the course of this book I've contended that human beings
have a desire for eternity. We look out into the starry sky at night
and wonder what it's all about. Why is there something rather than
nothing? Is there a creator of it all? If there is a God in the universe, we
seek to make a connection—like people trying to contact intelligent life
potentially existing on other planets. And yet, the desire for communication doesn't run in only one direction. I believe, as the ancient people of
Israel believed, that the God of the universe seeks us, calling out, in the
words of the book of Genesis, "Where are you?" The story of the Bible
is the tale of God seeking us out and calling us home.

Nowhere is this call more direct than in the person of Jesus Christ who the Christian tradition believes is God made flesh, the clearest and best mode of communication with humanity. This Jesus, through his ministry, death, and resurrection, seeks to be the true way that leads to life in a whole transformed creation—God's dream for the cosmos. This has been the Christian claim since the beginning.

The words of the Gospels and the whole New Testament are written not only as an account of the first witnesses to the life and work of Jesus, but also, as John's Gospel says, "that you may come to believe," or "that you may continue to believe." I think these different translations of the text are both true. Some of us have yet to come to belief; others need encouragement in continuing to believe.

Jesus's Invitation

As I discussed in the last chapter, the Gospel writers invite us to read the Gospel story with resurrection eyes—that is, to hear Jesus speaking not simply as the story of a young first-century prophet who met a tragic end, but as the risen Lord who speaks to each of us today. I've already discussed the stories in the Gospels where Jesus calls fishermen by the Sea of Galilee and invites them on a journey to follow him. Remember in John's Gospel, Jesus's first words to those who seek him are, "What are you looking for?" The voice of the risen Jesus is right here as you read these words. How do you respond?

When Jesus's first disciples ask where he is staying, he says "Come and see." But why would his disciples ask that question? The Greek word *meno*—to stay, dwell, or abide appears a total of thirty-three times in John's Gospel. The readers of this story who seek to follow Jesus are asking more than his street address. They want to know where the risen Jesus continues to abide. Later in John's story, Jesus invites his disciples to abide in him as he abides in them. It seems that Jesus abides in his disciples, in those who are part of his new creation. Jesus continues to abide in the flesh and blood of a new community of love that continues his mission in the world. We cannot know exactly what the future holds. Where will the Spirit of Jesus lead us? We are invited on a journey to come and see.

In another gospel story, Matthew, Mark, and Luke all tell us that Jesus asks his disciples who people say he is. The disciples report the various ideas people have about him. Then he asks the central question, "Who do you say that I am?" Simon Peter, one of Jesus's closest disciples, blurts out, "You are the Messiah, the Son of the living God." Again, while the Gospel writers tell a story about Jesus's mission in Galilee with his first disciples, the story behind the story is this: Peter saw and believed in Jesus's true mission, but when following Jesus got tough and Jesus was arrested and crucified, Peter ran away and denied him. After the Resurrection, when Jesus gave him the grace of forgiveness and when he received the power of the Holy Spirit in his life, Peter began to proclaim the message and the person of the one he recognized as Messiah. Jesus continues to ask this question through the pages of Scripture to you and me today, "Who do you say that I am?"

Over the centuries people have had varied answers to this question. Thomas Jefferson, the great American founding father, thought of Jesus as a great moral teacher. He even took a scalpel to the New Testament and literally cut out anything in the least miraculous or out of the ordinary. His Jesus was merely an itinerant philosopher proclaiming truths in keeping with his Enlightenment values. Others have seen him as the last in a line of great Jewish prophets, or one of many manifestations of the divine that have emerged in human history. The answer to Jesus's question is foundational as to what it means to be a Christian. We either believe what the Gospels say about him or we don't. The Gospels say he is the Messiah who died and rose from the dead and who inaugurated a whole new world order. This is the Christian claim about Jesus. A famous statement from C. S. Lewis says it best:

> You must make your choice. Either this man was, and is, the Son of God, or else a madman or something worse. You can shut him up for a fool, you can spit at him and kill him as a demon or you can fall at his feet and call him Lord and God, but let us not come with any

patronizing nonsense about his being a great human teacher. He has not left that open to us. He did not intend to.[1]

One of my mentors in the Christian life, Carol Anderson, has said that this decision we make about Jesus ought to be—and is—life changing. It isn't about becoming religious. It's about a relationship with a living Lord who invites us to turn around and follow him into the future.[2] At the same time, coming to believe in Jesus may not take place in a moment. It is most often a process. When Jesus invites us to follow him we start out from where we are one step at a time.

Each day I go to my gym I see a big sign: "Commit to Something." I believe that is what we all want to do. We want to invest in something worthwhile; maybe it's something as simple as a fitness goal, but I think that slogan resonates with people because it speaks to a deeper need we all have to make our lives matter, to commit to a greater purpose and a higher goal. That's what I think Christianity offers. That's why I have committed my life to be a disciple of Jesus Christ.

Pulled from the Matrix

During the Great Depression of the 1930s, President Herbert Hoover talked about American "rugged individualism." He meant that each of us should be able to use our own best efforts to pull ourselves "up by the bootstraps." This ideal still captures many of us. We think that if we can't take control of our own lives something must be wrong with us. We should be able to change ourselves and change the world around us by our own best efforts. I believe the idea of rugged individualism hasn't worked very well; ultimately it won't work.

We deceive ourselves into thinking we can become all we were meant to be on our own. People engaged in twelve-step programs get that reality more than those of us who haven't been on the bottom looking up. The twelve-step model tells the truth about being captured by addictions. We

---

1. Lewis, *Mere Christianity*, 51
2. Anderson and Summers, *Who Do You Say That I Am?*, 51–53.

are powerless to get out of them and we need a God to help us get out. We may think that's true for people with addictions, that's not our problem. But we can be addicted to many things—our careers, for example. We can struggle with issues of shame or a lack of forgiveness. Ultimately we will not escape death by our own power. We can't get rid of the fact that we fail to do the things we ought to do and do the things we wish we wouldn't do (Romans 7). Being caught in this reality, Paul cries out in exasperation, "Who will rescue me from this body of death?" He answers himself, "Thanks be to God through Jesus Christ our Lord."[3] For Paul and the Christian tradition, we can only get so far on our own steam. We need the pull of Christ to finally get beyond ourselves.

In our communal life, as I've discussed in chapter 3, all attempts to get ourselves "back to the Garden" have failed. There have been times when societies have done a good job advancing one program or another, but it seems whenever we improve society on one level, we go backwards on others. As I have already said, there is a whole network of personal and communal evil and social structures that constrain and hamper our efforts at social change. We can't escape the complex matrix on our own. We need the ultimate hope of new creation to make God's dream real for the world. In the meantime, we can create signs of the kingdom of God in the world, but we will never fully get there until the new world breaks into ours in fullness—that's what we mean by the second coming of Christ.

There is an Easter icon used in the Orthodox churches in which, having confounded the devil by dying on the cross, Jesus is depicted as grabbing the hands of Adam and Eve and pulling them out of the grave of the old world into the life of the new one. It is an amazing symbol of what Jesus does for us, snatching us out of the grip of the dark lord. Paul powerfully declares this reality when he says, "[God] rescued us from the control [power] of darkness and transferred us into the kingdom of the Son he loves."[4] If we make a decision to allow Christ to grab our hands, he plucks us from the dark powers and places us in a new kingdom. In

---

3. Rom. 7:24b–25.
4. Col. 1:13, CEB.

other words, we become citizens of another country while still living in the present one.

If we understand ourselves as being plucked out of the old order and citizens of the new, we come to understand the work we do as positive action to reclaim the world for the kingdom of God. The choices we make in the present world have eternal value, whether we choose to live for ourselves alone, or to live as we were created to be. Since the future world has already entered into the present one, we can plant seeds now for the new creation. A prayer composed in honor of the late martyred Archbishop Oscar Romero of El Salvador describes the reality of our work as Christians in the world:

> We accomplish in our lifetime only a tiny fraction of the magnificent enterprise that is God's work. Nothing we do is complete, which is a way of saying that the kingdom always lies beyond us . . .

This is what we are about.
We plant the seeds that one day will grow.
We water seeds already planted, knowing that they hold future promise.
We lay foundations that will need further development.
We provide yeast that produces far beyond our capabilities.
We cannot do everything, and there is a sense of liberation in realizing that.
This enables us to do something, and to do it very well.
It may be incomplete, but it is a beginning, a step along the way, an opportunity for the Lord's grace to enter and do the rest.
We may never see the end results, but that is the difference between the master builder and the worker.
We are workers, not master builders; ministers, not messiahs.
We are prophets of a future not our own.[5]

---

5. Composed by Bishop Ken Untener of Saginaw, drafted for a homily by Cardinal John Dearden in November, 1979, for a celebration of departed priests. United States Conference of Catholic Bishops website.

Born Again

What do you think about when you hear the words "born again"? You may think of Christians with heavy-handed evangelistic techniques trying to get you "saved." Often, hearing the words "born again" sounds like anything but good news. And yet, I hope we can recover those words just like the words "repent," or "evangelical," or even "saved." They are good words that have a wonderful meaning within the Christian tradition even though they have been hijacked by a vocal minority of Christians who I think have gone off track.

When I was fourteen years old, I went with my family to the Erie County Fair near Buffalo, New York, where I grew up. I was exploring on my own and in one of the exhibition halls beside the vegetable dicers and deluxe vacuum cleaners I found a booth where a woman sat with some Bibles and a sign with some Scripture verses on it. I was intrigued since I had never seen anything like it at my Roman Catholic church or school. The woman asked me if I was "born again." I didn't remember ever hearing that phrase before. I'm not sure what I said in response; I probably just gave her a puzzled look. She invited me to sit down and she went through several Bible verses explaining to me that I was a sinner and needed to be saved, to be born again in order to get to heaven. I went to Catholic school and church every Sunday. I had read the Bible, but I never had heard about this before. When she invited me to pray with her and invite Jesus into my heart, I thought, "Why not?" We prayed together and I said what some evangelicals call the "sinner's prayer" acknowledging that we have sinned, we are in need of salvation, and we accept Jesus as our personal Lord and Savior. I wasn't prepared, however for what happened in that experience. I had a sense of joy that's hard to describe in that moment. I think it might have been that, despite my religious training, I had never had the sense that Jesus was someone with whom I could have a relationship.

There's much about what I heard that day that I think now was totally off the mark. To tell somebody that all they have to do is say a prayer and they go to heaven is not what I understand to be the heart of Christianity. It's not what being "born again" means either. I will grant that I probably did not have a nuanced understanding of what that woman was talking about as a fourteen-year-old, but having spent time as a Pentecostal, it's not so far from the way a lot of folks understand what it means to "get saved." At the same time, I can't forget that experience of God's grace, love, and joy. I believe God had already claimed me as a beloved child before I went to the Erie County Fair. I have a deeper and richer understanding of what it means to be born again, and yet I also know that I came in touch with the Risen One that day in a way I had not experienced him before. I believe you can, too, if you haven't already, but let's explore in a fuller way what it really means to be born again.

That phrase appears in John's Gospel in the story of Jesus's encounter with Nicodemus, the same man who brought the extravagant amount of perfume and spice to anoint Jesus's body for burial. This is one of the beautiful mystical encounters that John recounts in some detail. Even though he tells this story early in the gospel, I hear the risen Jesus speaking not just to Nicodemus, but to all of us who listen in. Read this story. Then read it again.

> There was a Pharisee named Nicodemus, a Jewish leader. He came to Jesus at night and said to him, "Rabbi, we know that you are a teacher who has come from God, for no one could do these miraculous signs that you do unless God is with him."
>
> Jesus answered, "I assure you, unless someone is born anew, it's not possible to see God's kingdom."
>
> Nicodemus asked, "How is it possible for an adult to be born? It's impossible to enter the mother's womb for a second time and be born, isn't it?"
>
> Jesus answered, "I assure you, unless someone is born of water and the Spirit, it's not possible to enter God's kingdom. Whatever is born of the flesh is flesh, and whatever is born of the Spirit is spirit. Don't be surprised that I said to you, 'You must be born anew.' God's Spirit blows wherever it wishes. You hear its sound, but you don't know where it comes from or where it is going. It's the same with everyone who is born of the Spirit."
>
> Nicodemus said, "How are these things possible?"

Jesus answered, "You are a teacher of Israel and you don't know these things? I assure you that we speak about what we know and testify about what we have seen, but you don't receive our testimony. If I have told you about earthly things and you don't believe, how will you believe if I tell you about heavenly things? No one has gone up to heaven except the one who came down from heaven, the Human One. Just as Moses lifted up the snake in the wilderness, so must the Human One be lifted up so that everyone who believes in him will have eternal life. God so loved the world that he gave his only Son, so that everyone who believes in him won't perish but will have eternal life. God didn't send his Son into the world to judge the world, but that the world might be saved through him.[6]

This story has lots to chew on. It helps to think about this story as one first told orally in the gatherings of early Christians and among those who were wondering if they should embrace the message John was telling. As we read the story, we should not only hear John, but the risen Jesus speaking as well.

Nicodemus is a man in the dark. He comes to Jesus by night—a metaphor for his state of mind. He's a seeker even though he's a teacher and it's clear right from the start that he's pretty clueless about Jesus's message. When Jesus talks to Nicodemus he jumps right in with some pretty confusing stuff. Jesus doesn't thank Nicodemus for his kind acknowledgement. No small talk.

Jesus's words to Nicodemus remind me of the strange meeting between Jedi warrior Yoda and Luke Skywalker in the movie *The Empire Strikes Back*, or the Kung Fu master Po teaching the young "grasshopper" David Carradine in the old *Kung Fu* TV series where the teacher speaks in riddles not easily understood. "Unless someone is born anew (again) it's not possible to see God's kingdom." What does that mean? Here's the first place where words are more than what first meets

---

6. John 3:1–17, CEB.

the ear. John uses a word that in Greek can mean both anew/again or from above (*anothen*). John and Jesus want us to hear both things at once because the birth Jesus is talking about is rebirth. But it's not just being born—it's a birth that comes from God's kingdom and it is a birth into God's kingdom.

We may not get that at first; neither does Nicodemus. For him, his first birth is pretty good. After all he's a son of Abraham. He has the right religious pedigree. He's among the chosen. He's smart, he's secure, and he's a respected expert. So why is he in the dark and why does he visit Jesus in the first place?

"How can an adult be born?" he asks. How can you start all over? Or at least that's how I hear his words. I've often thought that Nicodemus would have loved to have started all over again. Nicodemus, and maybe all of us, wouldn't mind a new start to wipe the slate clean. But we can't do that. We can't be born again. What's done is done.

Jesus opens the door a little wider. "Unless someone is born of water and the spirit it's not possible to enter God's kingdom." The birth we all experience into this world is one reality. There's an opportunity though for the fresh start Nicodemus longs for. It takes place when we are plunged into the cleansing waters of baptism. It's as if we do start all over again. We are forgiven, we are clean. We are new. We are born into a new reality.

When we baptize babies in our congregation, we have the parents wrap them in a warm blanket, but underneath they are either naked or have only a little bathing suit on. We place them right down into the water and pour it over them as we say the words of baptism. Then we lift them up dripping from the font so the whole community sees them as they come out of the water. It's the clearest visual of what I'm talking about. It's as if they truly have just been born. Then we anoint their foreheads with perfumed oil and proclaim that they are sealed by the Holy Spirit in baptism and marked as Christ's own forever.

What about those of us who were baptized a long time ago? Do we need to be born again? Baptism is unrepeatable. I believe that whenever we are baptized we are marked as Christ's own forever. We already have been claimed by Christ. But we have to receive in our hearts what was done for us back then. We are invited to cultivate our covenant relationship with Jesus and claim our citizenship in the kingdom of God. We too can get a fresh start.

It doesn't matter how far we have wandered away. It doesn't matter what we have done or failed to do. We can leave guilt and shame behind, acknowledge that we have not been successful in trying to be our own savior, and ask forgiveness for what we've done. We don't have to continue carrying the heavy baggage we have been carrying for a long time: regrets, bad decisions, grudges, or whatever it may be. That's the amazing thing about grace—it means unmerited favor. God's grace is the crazy possibility that what goes around doesn't have to come around. We can be plucked out of the cycle of death and retribution. It changes the world.

Jesus's strange teaching gets a little stranger. "God's Spirit blows wherever it wants. You can hear it, but you don't know where it comes from or where it's going. It's the same with everyone born of the Spirit." John and Jesus remind us again of the creation story in Genesis where God's wind or breath swept over the waters. Jesus's image of God's Spirit is like that creative wind, this time bringing forth a new creation.

Once again, we have double meanings. The Greek word *pneuma* means spirit, breath, or wind. Remember when Jesus meets the disciples on the night of Easter, he breathes on them and gives them the Holy Spirit. We can maybe think, also, of the Spirit descending on Jesus in the River Jordan when he is baptized. The poetic images here tell us about the Spirit who is difficult to catch—like the wind, or like the risen Jesus himself. We experience him but we can't quite hold on to him. God's Spirit too dances around us and we can experience her presence, but can't hold on to her; she is blowing out into the world, joining our earthly reality with the heavenly one. It's that Spirit who is at work within the community of God's beloved children. It's that Spirit who works in us when we are baptized and transferred into the new creation.

"How are these things possible?" Nicodemus asks. The man speaks for all of us who find it difficult to see beyond material reality. How can we be born a second time? Can this be "real"? How is it possible? Jesus is speaking about a reality not easily grasped by what we can perceive by measuring, probing, examining. God's world has broken into ours and we can experience it, but it defies easy explanation.

Jesus then refers to a strange little story in the book of Numbers[7] in the Old Testament. As the people of Israel wander in the desert on their way to the Promised Land, they complain about how God is not taking care of them. Suddenly, poisonous snakes come into their camp and God tells Moses to make a bronze serpent and lift it up on a pole. Anyone who looks on the serpent will live. Jesus refers to this story as a reference to his crucifixion. Looking with faith at the bronze serpent healed the people of Israel. Looking at the crucified and risen Lord with faith will heal us as well. After all, we are people who have been poisoned by the serpent in the garden. We need a remedy to get us back on course.

The final portion of this story is perhaps the most famous passage in the New Testament. John tells us that since God loves this cosmos, God came in the flesh that whosoever believes in him might not die but have eternal life. When John uses that word, "cosmos," he means the world that's been under the control of the powers of death and sin. God loves the world that rebels against God. That's a powerful love: a love of the very world that sent Jesus to the cross. And that love seeks to welcome us back into the loving embrace of the father, just as the father welcomed the prodigal son in Luke's story.

To believe is to enter a covenant relationship, like the relationship Abraham had with God. It doesn't mean to give simple assent to a set of beliefs, but, instead, to say yes to Jesus's call to follow. It means we don't have to have it all sewn up. We don't have to understand it all. Like Nicodemus, Jesus is telling us that we don't have to know everything. We just have to go on the journey, to come and see where Jesus is going. "For God didn't send the Son into the world to judge or condemn the cosmos, but to save it," That's God's plan. God does not condemn us. God loves us. God does not condemn the world. God loves it and wants to restore it, remake it as he hoped from the beginning. And you and I are invited to be partners in new creation. Come and see!

---

7. Num. 21:4–9.

Covenant

Joining God's journey into the future requires commitment. We enter a covenant with one another and with God. In my tradition, the Episcopal Church, as well as other Christian traditions, that commitment comes in the form of the baptismal covenant. At the Great Vigil of Easter, those who will be baptized, their parents and godparents, those who will be received into the fellowship of the church who have already been baptized, along with the whole gathered community, renounce the powers of the world who seek to destroy the world and its creatures. We turn toward Jesus and we affirm, or reaffirm, the vows of the covenant.

As we discussed in chapter 4, a covenant is not a contract. It is an agreement to be part of a lifelong relationship. The vows we make in the baptismal covenant affirm our belief in the God of the Bible: the God who led Israel through the wilderness, the God who came to show us the way in Jesus, the God who continues to guide us into the future who we call Holy Spirit. We also affirm what we will do in response to that relationship: we will continue to be part of the community of God's beloved children, continue to remember the story of faith, pray together and celebrate the covenant meal, the Holy Eucharist. We will discuss that in more detail in the next chapter.

To be part of this community is essential to our covenant as Christians because, as we have said, Christianity is personal but not private. We aren't Christians on our own. We support one another in the community of believers. Remember, the risen Jesus showed up on that first Easter night in middle of his disciples. He still shows up through the Holy Spirit he breathes on them—and on us. Being part of that community also helps us to remember who we are. We need to hear the story. We need to celebrate together. We need encouragement to continue to live out our commitment to our covenant.

Finally, it doesn't end with us. The mission of Jesus is about the cosmos. We have the job of continuing the mission of loving and reclaiming the world. In our baptismal covenant we commit to proclaiming the good news of God's dream in what we say and what we do. We will look for and serve Christ wherever we see him, in the face of everyone we meet in the world, because he told us that whenever we serve those who are in need, we serve him.[8] And we commit to work to create signposts pointing toward the kingdom by working for social justice and peace, "respecting the dignity of every human being." Those vows are hard to live up to. That's why when we commit to them we say, "I will, with God's help." We are all in this together. We are God's partners in this project of reclaiming creation. God believes in us. So we press on toward the goal of God's total reclamation of the world. We believe that we are already part of that new creation. We are part of the community of those who have gone before us and who are here now. The writer of the Letter to the Hebrews[9] tells us we are in a long line of pilgrims going all the way back to Abraham who have always longed for a better country, a heavenly one. And God has prepared for us a future city where as it is in heaven so it will be on earth.

The medieval writer Peter Abelard penned a visionary hymn about the hope we share. He saw a city, as if in the distance, a new and perfected Jerusalem, not like the one we can visit today, but an image of God's perfect dream for human community. He uses our ancient Jewish experience of longing during the Babylonian exile, of hope for a return to our true Promised Land. We are not there yet. Whenever I sing this hymn I am moved to tears of joy and longing—like when I first set eyes on the Western Wall of the temple in Jerusalem. We are exiles, pilgrims, who still live in hope. If we have made a decision to "come and see," to follow Jesus into the new creation, this is our song as well:

> Now in the meanwhile, with hearts raised on high,
> We for that country must yearn and must sigh,
> Seeking Jerusalem, dear native land,
> through our long exile on Babylon's strand.[10]

---

8. See Jesus's powerful parable about the sheep and the goats in Matt. 25.

9. Heb. 11:1–16.

10. Peter Abelard, translated by John Mason Neale. The hymn text appears in many hymnals, including *The Hymnal 1982* of the Episcopal Church.

Questions for Reflection

1. At a key moment in the Gospels, Jesus turns to his disciples and asks: "Who do you say that I am?" How do you answer Jesus's question for your life?

2. When you hear the term "born again," what comes up for you? What about the word "grace"? Can these words have new meaning for us?

3. How is Christianity personal, but not private?

8

Church

What do you think about when you hear the word "church"? Does it mean a building for religious services like weddings or funerals? Is it an institution? Is it a congregation—maybe one you are or were part of? All of these, of course, are what "church" means to people. There are also associations the word brings up in our minds and hearts. Some people have been disappointed by churches. Some have been shunned. Some have been abused by congregations or by clergy. All these things are sadly true. And yet, church is the place many have found a community, or the place that is part of the fabric of their family or culture. Church can be both the place of rejection and guilt and the place of acceptance and unconditional love.

Throughout history, the institution of the Church has often failed to live up to its higher purpose. It has gone off course most often when it has colluded with the powers of the world and makes deals with the devil. The Church is composed of very fallible human beings who have sometimes turned away from their true calling as disciples of Jesus. All this is true. All this must be confessed if we are to be the Church Jesus calls us to be.

At the same time, when she has lived into her true self, the Church has been a leaven in society, achieving tremendous good both in the lives of individuals and whole cultures, despite what her detractors say. Think of the institutions of education, healing, and service to the poor all animated by the call of Jesus. Think of the social movements like those to abolish slavery in England and in the United States, the movement to end apartheid in South Africa, and the civil rights movement, to name a few. The fact remains that, despite the many failings of the Church through time, Jesus still calls human disciples to follow him in a community of faith. Paul calls us the Body of Christ—what a wonderful name for those whom Jesus has charged with continuing his mission in the world. And yet, as is all too painfully obvious, "But we have this treasure in clay jars, so that it may be made clear that this extraordinary power belongs to God and does not come from us."[1]

While the Church has an institution, she is not defined by the institution. Rather the Church is a mission and a movement: the Jesus movement with a mission to continue the work of the new creation in the world. The Church is composed of individuals, but it is not individualistic. It is a community on a pilgrimage through history, existing in many places. What are the ways she comes to know where the Holy Spirit is leading her in the world?

Creed

The Christian tradition developed language to describe and define the faith of Christians. These formulations are known as creeds. The most famous of these are the Apostles' Creed and the Nicene Creed, which emerged from an early church council. In that creed the Church is defined as one, holy, catholic, and apostolic.

To say the Church is "one" may seem pretty crazy on the face of it. There are all kinds of Christian churches. If we know anything about history, we know these various Christian "brands" have fought one another

---

1. 2 Cor. 4:7.

over who is right—sometimes literally fighting to the death. The stories of the Protestant Reformation and the Counter-Reformation in the sixteenth and seventeenth centuries are filled with such stories. They demonstrate not only our human failings, but how far off track we can get when we are beguiled by the logic of the dark forces of the world, and by using the tools of power, coercion, and violence to mistakenly advance a "good" cause.

Nevertheless, "Faith is necessarily a matter of perceiving the unseen in what can be seen."[2] The unity of the Church is our aspiration and our foundational reality. Unity is what we hope for; deep down it is our common identity as the Body of Christ. The Church is one in that it's joined to one Lord. There are not many bodies, just one.

Holiness is another aspiration for individual Christians and the Church as a whole. What is it to be holy? One definition is to be set apart for the use of God. Our goal is to be a positive force for the kingdom of God at all times. One implication of that is that we seek to become who we were created to be. Being holy is not about being "holier than thou." To be holy is to be transparent. To be genuine. To live in such a way that our true selves and our gifts as God created us shine through in our lives. That's what it means for the Church to be holy—we shine the light of Christ, live as the body of Christ, exist as the presence of Christ in all we say and do. Too often though, this sense of being "set apart" distances us from the world. Some Christians mistakenly understand themselves as being saved "from" the world rather than saved "in" the world and "for" the world. We're set apart to do the work of God, which is to transform the world, not escape it.

To be "catholic" is maybe the most misunderstood mark of the creed. When people hear that the Church is catholic they think it means Roman Catholic. But the Greek word *catholikos* means throughout the whole, or according to the whole, or universal. In that sense it means that the Church isn't in only one place, but exists throughout the world. The Church is like the mustard seed in Jesus's parable. Mustard is a tiny seed that grows into

---

2. Johnson, *The Real Jesus*, 254. Johnson's work is an excellent and fuller description of the elements of the Apostles' and Nicene Creeds.

a big shrub, but it's also prolific. It starts spreading here and there and it pops up where you least expect it. Christian communities arise in the least expected places sometimes and it's the job of Christians to permeate the world with the Church.

Another sense of being catholic is to receive and convey the faith of the Church across time and in every place. Again, there are Christians that have very different views of what Christianity is all about; there are even differences about the essentials. Yet, I think there are a few things that mark the faith of all Christians, as described in the two main creeds of the Church: the centrality of the Bible as our guiding text, the sacraments of Baptism and Eucharist (as I'll describe later), and our working for the kingdom of God.

To be catholic also means to be inclusive. The Church spans a wide diversity of historical epochs, cultures, and peoples. The Church isn't one kind of person in one kind of place, but all sorts of people and communities everywhere. That's the wonderful thing about the Church. At its best, it enculturates wherever it is while not losing its character of bringing the kingdom of God into the world. Our challenge is to discern between the richness of human diversity and what is destructive to human communities. At the same time, churches have too often given too high a value to things that are indifferent to the gospel and made them essential. For example, churches have too often mistaken European cultural norms as essential to Christianity. This is especially true when you look at churches built in Asia or Africa using Western architectural styles, looking like they dropped out of the English countryside, or the insistence of missionaries for indigenous people to adopt Western clothing and mores.

The vision of the Church as catholic is that of the great big party God wants for all eternity where everyone is welcome and invited as a beloved child. That vision can sometimes be challenging for us. In fact, many congregations are monochrome rather than multi-colored. We only get the benefit of being catholic when we seek out and invite the different perspectives and cultures of all kinds of people into our congregations. The standard operating procedure of the old world order is tribalism: keep others out. The beauty of God's kingdom is that we are bridge builders not wall makers.

What does it mean to be apostolic? First, it means to be faithful to the good news the first followers of Jesus—the apostles—proclaimed. It means to continue in the way of Jesus: what he taught and how he lived. It means to keep alive the hope of God's kingdom. Sometimes that means standing up for the authenticity of Christianity against not only its detractors, but also others who seek to change it or water it down. At the same time, we have to be able to discern the fresh ways the living Jesus is inviting us to travel. That is the give and take that has characterized the Church from the beginning and can result in rifts and squabbles as well as new life, energy, and growth.

While some Christian denominations would disagree with me here, the Church's apostolic ministry exists through the ongoing and living succession of the Church's leaders from the first apostles until now. Each generation of leaders, whom we call bishops, ordain the next to carry on their ministry through time. By laying their hands on the heads of their successors, as described in the Acts of the Apostles, bishops invite the gifts of the Holy Spirit for leadership and faithfulness to the Gospel to be handed on and safeguarded for the future. This succession from the apostles, I believe, is part of the essence of what it means to be the Church.

To be apostolic also means to be missionary. As I have said, the Church is a mission. Its whole purpose is to be what I call a demonstration project of the new creation in the world. Its mission is to reclaim the cosmos Jesus loves and died for. Only by being in the world and living as if the new creation is possible are we living into our identity as apostolic Christians. We live in a culture where Christianity is in decline. There are many people who have no idea what the essence of Christianity is all about. Each one of us who accepts life in Christ has a call to be apostolic. Each of us is a missionary in that we have the same mission the first apostles had—to tell someone else about what we experience as disciples of the risen Lord.

Word

How do we gain strength to be the Church in the world? How do we recharge our batteries? One way is to remember who we are through the words of the Bible. Here again, there is a lot of misunderstanding about what the Bible is and what role it has in the life of Christians. First and foremost, it's crucial to remember that the Word of God is a person, not a book. In the first chapter of his gospel, John tells us that the Word became flesh and lived among us: Jesus. The Word of God is a living person who directs us into the future and models the way we live. The risen Jesus does that in part by speaking to us through the words handed down to us by the writers of the Bible in their own languages, cultures, and time. It may be helpful to think about how we got the Bible, the New Testament in particular, since the Old Testament, or Hebrew Bible, had a much longer history of development.

Development of the New Testament

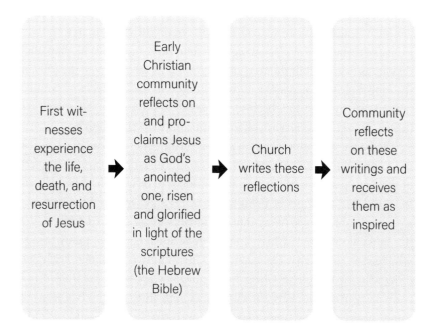

First witnesses experience the life, death, and resurrection of Jesus ➡ Early Christian community reflects on and proclaims Jesus as God's anointed one, risen and glorified in light of the scriptures (the Hebrew Bible) ➡ Church writes these reflections ➡ Community reflects on these writings and receives them as inspired

The chart above highlights the dynamic way the New Testament came to us. It is based, first of all, in the experience of the first disciples who walked with Jesus, went through the loss of his death, and then met him as the risen Lord. Those first Christians, the earliest community, met together and shared their experiences. They also reflected on those experiences in light of the Bible they knew, what we call the Old Testament, and used the language of those Scriptures to describe their experience of Jesus. That's why the story of Jesus walking with his disciples on the road to Emmaus on the first Easter is so compelling. The presence of the living Jesus helped those first followers understand the Bible in a new way in light of their experience. In a similar way, in John's Gospel Jesus tells us that the Holy Spirit will continue to help the Church reflect on what we experience and will lead us into truth.

The written forms of the New Testament began to appear after the early Church had told the stories of Jesus and lived the Christian life for a while. The first parts of the New Testament are the letters Paul wrote to the early Christian communities. Those letters describe the experience of being a Christian and the nature of the apostolic faith. It's only a bit later that the Gospels were written down, but the stories they embody had been told within the early Church for many years.

Finally, those written texts circulated throughout the early Church and were cherished as the message of the first generation of Christians. Slowly certain of those writings gained the status of authentic core texts that faithfully conveyed the message of the risen Lord. It wasn't until 367 CE that we have a list of the twenty-seven books currently in our New Testament in a letter from Athanasius, a well-respected bishop in Alexandria, Egypt. Even then, the books that compose our New Testament were those that the catholic (universal) church received as authoritative, not any external authority. In this sense it's crucial to remember the Bible is the book of the Church in that members of the living Church wrote it and received it as the definitive expression of its message. The Bible did not drop fully formed into the hands of the Church like Athena springing from the head of Zeus.

The text of the Bible the Church has received is a key place where we meet the risen Jesus who still challenges and comforts us through its words. We can meet him individually in our own meditation on the Scriptures and we can meet him when these words are proclaimed in the assembly of believers. He still comes into our midst like he did on the first Easter. We can meet him if we open our ears. Our relationship with the Scriptures is dynamic. We gain new insights as we read it in new contexts.

The chart below demonstrates the way the Bible works in the life of the Church through time and today.

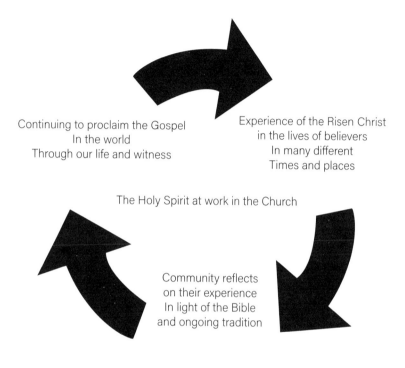

Continuing to proclaim the Gospel
In the world
Through our life and witness

Experience of the Risen Christ
in the lives of believers
In many different
Times and places

The Holy Spirit at work in the Church

Community reflects
on their experience
In light of the Bible
and ongoing tradition

We experience the risen Lord through the pages of the Bible, but also in our experience of his presence in the community of believers. Our experience assists us in proclaiming the Gospel in new ways in our own time and place, fueled and inspired by the Holy Spirit.

Sacraments

The English word "sacrament" is from a similar Latin word, but the early Church also used the Greek word *mysterion* or mystery to describe the rituals of the Christian community; that is a fruitful path to go down. What we celebrate in the two great sacraments of the Church, Holy Baptism and Eucharist or Holy Communion, is mysterious because while God acts within them, they are ultimately undefinable.

Growing up in the Roman Catholic Church, I was taught a sacrament is "an outward sign, instituted by Christ, to give grace." I didn't really understand what all that meant in second grade and maybe I still don't, or at least not completely. Because despite our human desire to define and dissect, there is a sense of the mysterious and the ineffable when we talk about God meeting us through physical signs that are meant to transform us. We can even say that the greatest physical way we can receive God's grace or unmerited favor to us is Jesus himself, God made flesh, God with skin on, who came among us as a person we could touch and see. Through his physical death and resurrection he opened up a whole new way of life for us. We can also talk about the Church as a sacrament since we are the Body of Christ continuing in the world as the vehicle by which God's grace comes into the world, although not the only one.

When we talk about sacraments we mean physical signs used dramatically to tell a story about God's action in our lives. Our participation in that ritual does something in our lives in a deeper, inner, spiritual way. All of that is to say that when we participate in a sacrament, God acts in our lives, even when we may not perceive it.

Baptism

We discussed in chapter 5 that the story of Jesus's baptism in the Jordan invites Christians to follow him through the water to new life. Throughout the New Testament, baptism is the way we can experience the new start promised in the Gospel. It's the means by which we are transferred from the powers of darkness and into the kingdom of God's beloved son. Paul talks a lot about baptism in his writing:

> Don't you know that all who were baptized into Christ Jesus were baptized into his death? Therefore, we were buried together with him through baptism into his death, so that just as Christ was raised from the dead through the glory of the Father, we too can walk in newness of life. If we were united together in a death like his, we will also be united together in a resurrection like his. This is what we know: the person that we used to be was crucified with

him in order to get rid of the corpse that had been controlled by sin. That way we wouldn't be slaves to sin anymore, because a person who has died has been freed from sin's power. But if we died with Christ, we have faith that we will also live with him. We know that Christ has been raised from the dead and he will never die again. Death no longer has power over him. He died to sin once and for all with his death, but he lives for God with his life. In the same way, you also should consider yourselves dead to sin but alive for God in Christ Jesus.[3]

He tells us that by undergoing this baptismal drama, we spiritually die to the old cosmos and are reborn in the new creation. We become citizens of another country, God's beloved children. He then challenges us to live like it—to have lifestyles reflecting our holy status. That's the hard part. In his Letter to the Galatians he goes on to say:

All of you who were baptized into Christ have clothed yourselves with Christ. There is neither Jew nor Greek; there is neither slave nor free; nor is there male and female, for you are all one in Christ Jesus. Now if you belong to Christ, then indeed you are Abraham's descendants, heirs according to the promise.[4]

There's a sense in which in baptism we exchange our old clothes—clothes of a slave, clothes of the wanderers, clothes like the prodigal made dirty by slopping the hogs—and we are washed and dressed for a banquet. Remember what the father says to the younger son in Jesus's parable, "Bring the best robe and put it on him, put a ring on his finger and sandals on his feet . . . because this son of mine was dead and has come back to life! He was lost and is found!"

The early Church celebrated baptism with the rich use of symbols to tell the story of what was happening to the new Christian. First, the candidates for baptism faced west and were asked to renounce all the principalities and powers that sought to hold God's creatures in bondage. Then

3. Rom. 6:3–11, CEB.
4. Gal. 3:27–29, CEB.

they were asked to turn to the east, the direction of the rising sun and the direction of Eden, the place of our first home with God. They would strip off their old clothes and walk down into the water of the baptismal font where the bishop would baptize them in them in the name of the Father, Son, and Holy Spirit. They would emerge on the other side to be clothed in a clean white robe and anointed with a perfumed oil called *chrism*.

All these symbols reinforce the truth that the newly baptized person was being transferred from one realm and into another. They left the land of slavery and wilderness-wandering on one side of the font and came up the other side like the people of Israel entering the Promised Land. They went down into the water as if they were drowned into death with Jesus, but they came up on the other side sharing in Jesus's Resurrection. New white clothes represented forgiveness of all that was past. In baptism, we are washed clean and have a new life in a new community. Oil in the ancient world was used to prepare someone for celebration. It also was used by athletes to prepare for competition. In the Old Testament it signaled the beginning of a new vocation, especially for prophets and royalty.

Symbols, songs, words, and actions all richly tell the Christian story. It's like a play being performed. We call this liturgy, but we might also call it dramaturgy—a word actors use for the performance of a play, the acting out of the story. All of us in the community of the Church who gather around the newly baptized participate in this drama. We all participate as actors because we all share in this same life in Christ. In many churches, we all renew our baptismal vows as part of the event of baptism, especially when we celebrate the sacrament at Easter, the great day of Resurrection.

We may wonder then why infants are often baptized. Maybe you were baptized as a small child and have no memory of it. We know in the early Church that whole households of people were baptized at once when a family converted to Christianity. In the early Church, people who became Christians typically were making a decision to convert from the pagan religions of the Roman Empire. It is appropriate to baptize infants and children, because what we do in baptism is always the work of God and not us. It is a gift of God's grace to claim us as citizens of the new creation, so why not bring our children into the new community of God's household? Nevertheless, we have to make an adult decision to receive that grace for ourselves, to claim our heavenly citizenship. That's why, over time, there emerged in the Church's history another rite called confirmation, to allow each of us publicly to affirm our faith in the midst of the community of God's beloved.

Baptism of children brings up another facet of baptism. It is a sign of the new covenant. Remember in the Old Testament God gave Abraham the physical sign of circumcision. All the male children of Israel were circumcised when they were eight days old. They became children of the covenant before they could accept or reject it. Baptism serves also as a sign of that covenant whereby we are sealed by the Holy Spirit and marked as Christ's own forever—not only males, but females as well. Paul's radically inclusive message was that there exists no more gender distinctions, no more tribal distinctions, no more economic or class distinctions to separate us in this new reality. All of us are part of the New Covenant. In this radical ritual, we accept the covenant God has made with us in the life and death and resurrection of Jesus, to claim us as God's own. No matter who we have been, God says yes to us, and we say yes to God. You and I are beloved. We are worthy.

Eucharist

In about the year 55 CE, Paul wrote one of his letters to the Christians in the Greek city of Corinth. He provides what is probably the earliest reference to the Lord's Supper in the New Testament:

> I received a tradition from the Lord, which I also handed on to you: on the night on which he was betrayed, the Lord Jesus took bread. After giving thanks, he broke it and said, "This is my body, which is for you; do this to remember me." He did the same thing with the cup, after they had eaten, saying, "This cup is the new covenant in my blood. Every time you drink it, do this to remember me." Every time you eat this bread and drink this cup, you broadcast the death of the Lord until he comes.[5]

---

5. 1 Cor. 11:23–26, CEB.

Paul writes about the oral tradition already being handed down, about the performance of a story. On the night before he died, Jesus took bread, said the blessing, broke it, and said, "This is my body." Then he took the cup and said, "This is the new covenant in my blood." He said to do this action to remember him. In so doing, we proclaim the death and resurrection of the Lord in word and action.

Paul handed on this tradition roughly twenty years after the events they recall. What we have come to call Holy Communion, the Eucharist, or the Mass was celebrated in a very early form from the earliest days of the Christian Church. How does this sacramental meal fit into our lives as Christians? Whole treatises have explored and expounded what the Eucharist means—a word that simply means "thanksgiving" in Greek. It refers to both the prayer of thanksgiving prayed over the bread and wine and the offering of thanks we make for the gift of the life, death, and resurrection of Jesus whom we receive at the Lord's Table. Philosophical arguments have parsed the way in which Christ is present in the sacrament—or not. Many a fight has been fought over this sacrament of unity of all things! Yet, the foundation of what needs to be said about the sacrament of the Lord's Body and Blood is given to us by Paul in First Corinthians.

"I received a tradition from the Lord . . . handed on to you," Paul begins. This tradition Paul hands on was first handed on from Jesus himself who first performed the story. He invites us to continue using his own words and deeds. Jesus hands on this tradition to the first apostles and to Paul and they hand it on to generations of Christians, and now we will hand it on to the next generation. That handing on is crucial, not only in the sacrament, but also in the handing on through time of who we are— the living Body of Christ in the world. We hand that identity down not just through a set of beliefs, but, primarily, through a living community of faith. A people of the New Covenant. You and I are part of that great chain that exists from the first Christians to us.

Remember what I said about dramaturgy, that wonderful word from the world of theatre. What I love about it is that it blends the word "liturgy," the word we use for sacred rituals, with the word "drama." The actions we perform in the sacraments tell the story they are meant to convey. The word dramaturgy also found its way into sociology through the work of the eccentric sociologist Erving Goffman who believed that all of life is the learning of roles that we play. We are socialized in those roles by those who go before us. We learn the dramas from them. Jesus and Paul handed on the dramaturgy of the Eucharist to us. What's also key here is that there are no observers, only performers in this drama. There is one who says the words of Jesus and performs the ritual actions of taking, blessing, breaking, and giving, but we all participate in the drama.

What are we "proclaiming" in this dramaturgy? Paul says it's the Lord's death until he comes again. But it isn't only Jesus's death, because it is a proclamation until he comes again, which means it also is about his life right now in the world and in us. What this drama proclaims, then, is that Jesus gave his body and poured out his blood as one of us—as a human—so that he could take our humanity into the new creation so that where he is we may be also.

He says, "This bread is my body, this wine is my blood. Take it and eat and drink; let my life be in you and you in me." Those last words come from the fifteenth chapter of John's Gospel when Jesus says he is a vine and we are the branches. "Abide in me and I in you," he tells us. One physical way we do that is by receiving his body and blood in the Eucharist.

What, then, are we receiving? Wars of words and even actual wars were fought in part over this question during the Reformation. Roman Catholics insisted that the bread and wine of the Eucharist were simply the forms under which the true body and blood of Christ were received. Some Protestants said that the bread and wine were simply a means to help remember Jesus's body and blood and nothing more. It seems to me that we get into problems when we are tempted to precisely define how Jesus is present in the sacrament. Yet, I think it is absolutely clear that what we receive is in fact the presence of the living Lord, his Body and Blood. I can't say any more than that. I don't need to.

To reflect on that mystery—remember that's what sacraments are called in Greek—we have to go back to the mystical Gospel of John. When he tells the story of the Last Supper he leaves out the story Paul tells. The other three Gospel writers tell us a similar story as Paul, but not John. Instead, he tells us about Jesus getting up from the table and washing his disciples' feet. But John talks a lot about the meaning of the

Eucharist, just not where we might expect it. He talks about it after Jesus feeds the five thousand.

> "I am the bread of life. Your ancestors ate the manna in the wilderness, and they died. This is the bread that comes down from heaven, so that one may eat of it and not die. I am the living bread that came down from heaven. Whoever eats of this bread will live forever; and the bread that I will give for the life of the world is my flesh."
>
> The Jews then disputed among themselves, saying, "How can this man give us his flesh to eat?" So Jesus said to them, "Very truly, I tell you, unless you eat the flesh of the Son of Man and drink his blood, you have no life in you. Those who eat my flesh and drink my blood have eternal life, and I will raise them up on the last day; for my flesh is true food and my blood is true drink. Those who eat my flesh and drink my blood abide in me, and I in them. Just as the living Father sent me, and I live because of the Father, so whoever eats me will live because of me. This is the bread that came down from heaven, not like that which your ancestors ate, and they died. But the one who eats this bread will live forever."[6]

Jesus's words as John relates them are very clear about the physical flesh and blood Jesus gives us. In fact, the Greek sense of these words is even more graphic. The word we translate as "eat" is the Greek word *phage*, which carries the idea of eating heartily, or devouring. And when John talks about "feeding on his flesh," he uses the word *trōgōn*, to gnaw on or munch on.

The Jewish leaders, like Nicodemus whom we encountered in the last chapter, take Jesus's words too literally. We may be tempted to similarly misunderstand his words. Jesus is not inviting us to physically gnaw on his human body or imbibe his physical blood. At the same time, Jesus's words help us to avoid over-spiritualizing his presence. Jesus, the Risen One, speaking through the pages of the Gospel tells us that when we receive him in the sacrament, we are encountering his real and physical and risen

---

6. John 6:48–58.

presence. We touch him and he touches us; we become part of him and he becomes part of us.

When we perform this dramaturgy we experience those next to us and near us—perhaps very different from us, perhaps similar—each receiving the presence of the same Lord at the same table. Like the feeding of the five thousand, everyone receives what they need if we only open our hearts. As this bread and wine is transformed in the dramturgy of communion, our everyday, embodied selves can be transformed, forgiven, healed. The living, fleshly, embodied Christ comes to each of us. The English spiritual writer Esther De Waal challenges us to see what Jesus asks of us in response:

> The Gospel confronts me with the whole Christ, and the whole
>   Christ demands the whole woman, the whole man.
> Christ loves the whole woman, the whole man.
> Christ wants the whole woman, the whole man.
> Christ loves and wants the whole of me, not the counterfeit self, not
>   the pretend self, not the half self.[7]

When we meet the fleshly Christ in his risen body and blood, we meet the whole Christ who knows us without our masks. He sees beyond our shame or pretensions. He meets us as we are.

Then, as Jesus meets us and we him, we get up and leave that place. Remember on the first Easter the first disciples met the risen Lord behind closed doors? Obviously, they didn't stay there. They went out into the world and started to proclaim what they experienced. That's the story of Pentecost in the Acts of the Apostles. When the Holy Spirit fills the hearts of his first disciples it's like thunder and fire and they can't contain themselves. They have to go out into the world and begin to live the life of the new creation while still being in the old order. When we receive the body and blood of Jesus, we need to see that we are what we eat and then go out and continue the Jesus mission in our everyday lives as he has come to us in our everyday lives energized by the power of the Holy Spirit. "We do

---

7. De Waal, *Living with Contradiction*, 43.

not return to the world to honor a dead man who once lived; we re-enter the world to let the Christ who now lives extend his living in the world through us."[8]

Other Sacraments

Over the course of the life of the Church, other sacramental rites emerged. I've already mentioned confirmation as one of those. Christians differ as to what ritual experiences count as sacraments. At the same time, I think Jesus meets us in a myriad of ways to give us grace, so I'm not too concerned about trying to over-define what is and isn't a sacrament. That being said, the first of these other sacramental rites is called confession or, more properly, reconciliation. When Jesus meets his disciples on the first Easter evening he breathes on them and says, "Receive the Holy Spirit. If you forgive anyone's sins they are forgiven; if you don't forgive them, they aren't forgiven."[9] Jesus's living Spirit enlivens the Church to be his ongoing, embodied presence in the world. That includes absolving people's sins—announcing to you and to me that in Christ we are forgiven. When we mess up and turn away from the direction of God's ways we can be forgiven again and again. What's also key here is that forgiveness is communal. Jesus gives the Church the power to pronounce that forgiveness.

As a priest, I have had amazing experiences in which I have pronounced that absolution and known the wonderful sense of forgiveness and release people experience in that sacramental moment. To be clear, I'm not doing it. It is the presence of the risen Jesus giving his grace to the person in the sacrament. I have experienced release and forgiveness as well. That doesn't mean that we can't ask for forgiveness on our own. Of course, we can. But there is something about hearing those words of forgiveness proclaimed by another person that can make a difference, especially when we have been carrying around guilt or shame, sometimes for a very long time.

8. Vogel, *Radical Christianity*, 124.
9. John 20:22b–23, CEB.

But why would Jesus say the sins you don't forgive, won't be forgiven? It seems to me that has to do with true contrition. In other words, we are mistaken if we believe that God's grace is cheap, that we can engage in things that draw us into ourselves and away from God and simply expect we will be forgiven if it doesn't involve a change of heart. God's grace is costly. Jesus gave his life for our reconciliation. If that's so, then we have to be serious when we ask to be restored to that right relationship. We have to desire to amend our lives to get back on track.

A second of the other sacramental rites is ordination. As I have said, one of the distinctive marks of the Church is that it is apostolic. In part, that means we hand on to the next generation the good news of the Gospel we have received. A tangible way we express that reality is through "laying on hands." In the New Testament, the apostles lay their hands on those they ordained for ministry as a physical demonstration of handing on the mission from one person to the next. In the history of the Church, this tactile way of authorizing ministry has continued until today. In my tradition, as in many of the historic denominations, we believe that this apostolic succession is given primarily to bishops, as visible symbols of apostolic authority and of unity in the Church. This is in keeping with ancient tradition from the earliest centuries of Christianity.

A third sacramental rite is anointing the sick for healing. The Letter of James says, "Are any among you sick? They should call for the elders of the church and have them pray over them, anointing them with oil in the name of the Lord. The prayer of faith will save the sick, and the Lord will raise them up; and anyone who has committed sins will be forgiven."[10] Once again, the ministry of Jesus to heal is extended through the Body of Christ in the world. The healing of sickness is also related to forgiveness; sickness in body is related to sickness of the soul. Both can be healed by God's power. Of course, healing comes in many ways. Even death can sometimes be a blessed release and a healing. At the same time, physical healings do happen, sometimes beyond our ability to understand. Healing prayer accompanied by anointing with oil is an ancient sacramental

---

10. James 5:14–15.

practice in the Church. It highlights the care Jesus invites us to take with one another. To help, to touch, to heal, to reach out our hands in love and extend Jesus's ministry. Here is a great poem written by the mystic St. Theresa of Avila:

> Christ has no body but yours,
> No hands, no feet on earth but yours,
> Yours are the eyes with which he looks
> Compassion on this world,
> Yours are the feet with which he walks to do good,
> Yours are the hands, with which he blesses all the world.
> Yours are the hands, yours are the feet,
> Yours are the eyes, you are his body.
> Christ has no body now but yours,
> No hands, no feet on earth but yours,
> Yours are the eyes with which he looks with
> compassion on this world.
> Christ has no body now on earth but yours.

The healing ministry and the sacrament of anointing clearly demonstrate this profound truth about the mission of the Church in the world.

The fourth sacramental rite in the tradition of the Church is Christian marriage. Of all the rites whereby we meet Christ embodied, this is perhaps the clearest. Jesus uses a wedding as the symbol of the eternal wedding feast of the new creation when, in John's Gospel, he performs a miracle of extravagant abundance by changing water into wine. When two people enter into a covenant of marriage, as I discussed in chapter 4, they are in a sense committing to be Christ for one another in good times and in bad, until they are parted by death. This is a sacrament that two people confer on one another and it isn't conferred only on the day of their wedding. The ritual moment happens when the minister representing the Church points to the two people and essentially says, "Look! Here is a sacrament of Christ's love right before our eyes." The couple becomes an icon, a symbol of Christ's love for all of us. No marriage does that perfectly, yet even in the imperfections, the light of that love can give us hope in a world where true covenant love is so difficult to find.

One of the great things about Christian marriage is that in many cases it provides the place where we nurture our children. The love between parents and children is also a sacramental sign of God's love for us and our dependence on the providence and love of God in our lives. This is all to say that the love of members of a family is one of the best ways we convey Christ's love to one another. Families may take all different forms, including households of people who have found family together even though they are not physically related. Even monastic communities can live out the sacramental nature of covenant love for one another. And yet, we also know that we love imperfectly. Marriages and families, although having the potential to be living signs of love, often fall short. Maybe that's where grace, forgiveness, and reconciliation come back in view.

While these various sacramental rites have a long tradition in the Church, Jesus meets us with his grace in all sorts of ways. When I look at the starry skies or glimpse the beauty of the natural world I have the opportunity to perceive the grace of God. When friends or family share a meal and the food and conversation transcend simple eating and drinking, Jesus is there as the unseen guest. When Christians reach out their hands in mission in the world, through social justice or acts of mercy, a sacramental moment happens.

When we gather on the Thursday of Holy Week, before the celebration of Easter, called Maundy Thursday, we celebrate our Lord's "mandate" or command to his disciples. The word "maundy" comes from the old English word for mandate. John's Gospel tells us that Jesus got up from the table at the last supper. He tied an apron around him and began to wash his disciples' feet, the job of a slave, not a rabbi. He says to us, "I have given you an example that so you also should do." All of us get up from our places and wash each other's feet. We do this dramaturgy as a sign of how we are supposed to live our lives in doing mercy, justice, and service to one another and to the world and to the earth as God's creation. I believe in the beauty of that poignant moment as we celebrate our Lord's presence with us and as we are present again with him at his last supper, we receive the strength, encouragement, and grace from our Lord himself to do the work he has given us to do. It's profoundly sacramental. In the words of the Latin hymn that has been sung during the washing of feet for well over a thousand years, "Ubi caritas et amor, Deus ibi est." Where there is charity and love, God is there.

Quo Vadis Domine?

An old story says that when Jesus's disciple Peter was an old man and bishop of Rome during the persecution of the emperor Nero, he decided to leave town rather than face crucifixion or a death in the arena. As he was on the Apian Way outside Rome, he met Jesus, but Jesus was carrying a cross. Peter called out to him, "Quo vadis Domine?" "Where are you going, Lord?" Jesus answered that he has to go to Rome and be crucified again with his brothers and sisters because his friend and disciple Peter had deserted his flock. Peter got the message. He returned to Rome where he met his death by crucifixion, but, unlike his Lord, tradition says he asked to be crucified upside down.

This tale about Peter not only helps us remember that Jesus walks with us as his Body through glory and through persecution. It also reminds us that Jesus goes out ahead of us leading us into the future, pointing the way. The Church continually asks Jesus the question Peter asked, "Where are you going, Lord?"

Peter's question reminds me of the dialogue between Jesus and his disciples in John's version of the Last Supper:

> "Do not let your hearts be troubled. Believe in God, believe also in me. In my Father's house there are many dwelling places. If it were not so, would I have told you that I go to prepare a place for you? And if I go and prepare a place for you, I will come again and will take you to myself, so that where I am, there you may be also. And you know the way to the place where I am going." Thomas said to him, "Lord, we do not know where you are going. How can we know the way?" Jesus said to him, "I am the way, and the truth, and the life. No one comes to the Father except through me."[11]

---

11. John 14:1–6.

How can we know the way into the future? We can have an idea of how Jesus led his first disciples, but the world is complex. Our cultural, political, and social situations are different from Judea in the first century. We may know ultimately that we are on our journey home, but like Thomas we ask, how do we know the way? How do we know where Jesus is going?

Jesus says he is the way, the truth, and the life. Throughout the last several chapters I've described how we know that we can find life in him as our risen Lord. We believe that his way truly leads us home. We even know that he is the example of how we should live our lives—he is the way into the future. Still, how do we follow him through our culture, in our time?

As I see it, there is a balance of several elements that help us discern our way into the future. First, Scripture is the faithful telling of the story and the reflections of the early community of believers. Both the story of the Jewish people in the Hebrew Bible and the story of the New Testament tell us where we have been; those stories help us go forward as well. But as we look back, we also see where Christians have travelled for two millennia. There is a rich tradition of spiritual travelers who have walked the road before and point the way ahead. Things we may have thought are new to our place and time, we can sometimes see have also been faced by others who have gone before us. And both of these need to be evaluated in the light of our reason. That means we need to contextualize the wisdom of the past in light of our present reality. We can use the knowledge at our disposal, including the knowledge of science, history, criticism, sociology, psychology, and all the other branches of knowledge we might need to help us to understand the present and understand the Scriptures and tradition as we discern our way as faithful disciples of Jesus.

Finally, there is experience. How do we as the Church in the twenty-first century experience the risen Lord? What does he say to us in our hearts and mind? When we meet him in the sacraments, when we meet him in the word of Scripture, when we meet him in the community of other beloved disciples as we ponder how we act in the world, there we will see him. He goes before us mapping the trail ahead if we open our hearts and spiritual eyes and ears.

The Holy Spirit will lead us as we discern our way ahead traveling home. The Spirit acts through the gifts we each have as members of the Body of Christ. Each of us is invited to share our skills, our insights, and our spiritual gifts to build one another up and to support each other in our growth in Christ. Together we discern our way as pilgrims. That's why there is no Lone-Ranger Christianity. We are all in this together, as parts of one body. That's what it means to be the Church. That's what it means to be Christ in the world.

Questions for Reflection

1. What have been your experiences of church in your life?
2. How does the Holy Spirit continue to guide the Church in many different times and places?
3. How does the experience of baptism in the early Church influence your understanding of baptism? What does new life in Christ mean for you?
4. Sacraments are outward and visible, material signs that convey deeper spiritual realities. How do you experience God through physical things?
5. Does the Eucharist have a deep meaning for you? If so, can you describe it?

9

Practice

Your way of acting should be different from the world's way; the love of Christ must come before all else.
— Rule of St. Benedict 4:20–21

Winston Churchill once quipped, "They say that nobody is perfect. Then they tell you practice makes perfect. I wish they'd make up their minds." Despite Mr. Churchill's witty remark, both things are true. We strive for perfection and we all make mistakes. Still, the only way we can become what we want to be is through practicing day in and day out. That's true for anyone that makes it look easy—singers, actors, athletes all practice. They have faith and hope that they will achieve their goal and they love what they do, so they are willing to discipline themselves to keep going even when it's hard.

The same is true about being a practicing Christian. We may never get it perfect, but we keep practicing. Benedict, the great founder of Western monasticism, founded his monasteries as "schools for the Lord's service." He understood that the Christian life can only be lived by the daily discipline of practice. His rule for monks and nuns offers practical guidelines on how to live. I think each community of Christians should see itself as a school for the Lord's service. We are always practicing and it's only in the day-by-day living out of our life in Christ that we will slowly become who God created us to be.

Each of us determines what we do with what we have all the time within the constraints of our lives. We have twenty-four hours a day to spend. Nobody has any more than that. We all have talents and skills. We have a certain amount of resources. We probably have obligations of work, or school, and family. What we do with what we have is a matter of priorities. Benedict lays before us a challenge to make the love of Christ come before all else. If we do that, our lifestyle will look different from that of those caught up in the matrix of this world. Christianity is counter-cultural. That's not just for monks; it's for all of us.

In the Roman Empire in which Paul lived, athletes were celebrities and athletic games like the Olympics were very popular, maybe not so different from our world. Paul uses athletic metaphors to encourage his fellow Christians to engage in the discipline of the Christian life:

> You've all been to the stadium and seen the athletes race. Everyone runs; one wins. Run to win. All good athletes train hard. They do it for a gold medal that tarnishes and fades. You're after one that's gold eternally. I don't know about you, but I'm running hard for the finish line. I'm giving it everything I've got. No sloppy living for me! I'm staying alert and in top condition. I'm not going to get caught napping, telling everyone else all about it and then missing out myself.[1]

We are training to become what we were created to be, reflecting the image of Christ in our lives. Let's run to win. Like excellent athletes we need to practice Christianity daily, and over time. The more we practice, the less we will conform to the patterns of the old world, and the more transformed we will be into citizens of the new creation.

---

1. 1 Cor. 9:24–27, MSG.

As the old saying goes, Rome wasn't built in a day. Christian practice is not about being holier than thou; it's about engaging in ways of living that will make your life fuller and more meaningful by walking in the wisdom of the way of Jesus. There are all sorts of specific practices that have emerged out of our Christian tradition to help us live more abundant lives. I present a few for you to consider. There's no need for shaming and blaming or even perfection for that matter. As one old monk once described the Christian life, "We fall and we get up. We fall and we get up again." These practices are interrelated. Some practices that I describe as personal have communal dimensions. Practices that are communal may also have missional dimensions. Of course, that's because we are holistic people who live in multiple dimensions.

DYNAMIC RELATIONSHIP OF PRACTICES TO TRANSFORM INDIVIDUALS, COMMUNITIES AND THE WORLD

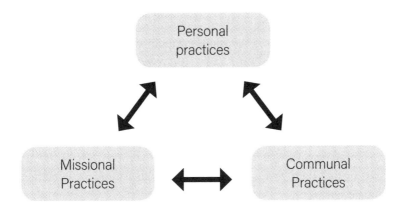

Personal Practices

Personal practices are those that have to do with our individual and family life. How do we live at work and home? What do we eat? How do we choose to spend our money, or our leisure time? These are all questions related to the Christian life. Our spiritual life is connected to our physical life. William Temple, a famous archbishop of Canterbury, wrote that Christianity "is the most avowedly materialistic of all the great religions." He didn't mean that we are people who value material things above all else. He meant that Christ comes to us in the flesh, as human, and in the ordinary, the physical things of life. The practices I discuss here are examples of ways we can practice our personal faith. Of course, the communal and missional practices also have personal dimensions, as I noted above. The goal of all these practices is transformation. We seek to reflect more clearly the face of Christ as individuals and as communities of faith in the world. We begin with prayer, the foundational practice of the Christian life.

Prayer

Developing a relationship with God is the essence of prayer. If we want to get to know someone we need to spend time with them. A discipline of daily prayer is a crucial spiritual practice. But there are all sorts of prayer practices, so experimentation about what works for you is key.

We can't forget that Jesus himself taught us a model for prayer in the familiar words we call the Lord's Prayer. The words of this prayer have infused themselves into my life. As I have the opportunity to minister to people at the end of life, or with those whose memories are failing, I'm always surprised how the words of this prayer are planted deep within people who have learned them and said them throughout their lives. Familiarity, though, can sometimes make us lose sight of the depth of meaning in these words, so let's focus on them using a contemporary language version:

> Our Father in heaven,
> hallowed be your Name,
> your kingdom come,
> your will be done,
> on earth as in heaven.
> Give us today our daily bread.
> Forgive us our sins
> as we forgive those

who sin against us.
Save us from the time of trial,
and deliver us from evil.
For the kingdom, the power,
and the glory are yours,
now and for ever.[2]

The first words acknowledge God as Jesus does: as his father and ours. Other versions of this prayer emphasize God as Father and Mother, and those images may indeed resonate with us. Mothering images of God are part of the Bible. The central idea is to realize our relationship with God is as parent and child. Jesus used the word "Abba" to relate to God.

As I was riding on a train from Newark airport into Manhattan once, I saw a young Jewish family. The father held a beautiful baby boy in his arms and their eyes were fixed on one another. As he rocked the baby back and forth, he kept saying, "Abba, Abba." The experience of love and connection clearly shown between parent and child was what Jesus meant when he said abba, when he spoke to his father. That's how God sees us as beloved children. That's what the Lord's Prayer asks us to think about when we say "our Father." Notice that it's not "my" but "our." It's not just an individual relationship, but one that even Jesus acknowledged was communal—a family connection. We are all part of that same family; we are our siblings' keepers because we have one loving parent who gives and sustains all life.

First, we acknowledge the intimacy of God, then we acknowledge the majesty of God who is the creator of all things, the Lord of the universe. We also acknowledge that there is a reality, a dimension beyond this one, where God reigns. We live in a world where the kingdom has broken in but is not yet fully here. We know there is another dimension that exists beyond our vision, but not beyond our experience. We pray, your kingdom come, your will be done perfectly in this world as it is in the heavenly dimension. May these two worlds become one. May this world

---

2. The Book of Common Prayer, 1979, 97.

be transformed. It is a statement of faith and hope. It is also a statement of our resolve to claim this world for the kingdom of heaven.

Then we ask for what we need and for what all people need. We realize our right relationship with our creator and sustainer—the one from whom all our blessings flow. We acknowledge our need and that of others and in so doing acknowledge that we are our siblings' keeper.

We go further and acknowledge our connection with God and one another when we ask to be forgiven as we forgive. That's a sure sign of the kingdom of God—the presence of forgiveness and grace. Jesus invites us to receive the gift of newness, of forgiveness, of starting over, and invites us to do the same. In all our relationships, may we forgive others for the hurt we have experienced. May we restore broken relationships, to the degree we have the power to do so.

The next phrase is more confusing: "Lead us not into the time of trial," or temptation, as the traditional version puts it. Have you ever had a time of trial in your life? I have had dark times, times of self-doubt, times of loss and heartbreak, times when I felt alone, times I wondered if there was a God. I'm sure you have had times of trial. When we get to the other side of these trials we can see how they may have brought us growth or healing, but it's not fun going through them. We ask, "If it's possible, keep us from it. Deliver us from evil. Keep us safe." Yet, when Jesus went through the greatest trial of his life in the Garden of Gethsemane before his arrest, he placed himself in his Father's hands: "Not my will but yours be done." We might add, on earth as it is in heaven. Ultimately, we acknowledge our dependence on our God whom we believe loves us and we trust in God's providence because the kingdom and power and glory are God's now and forever.

Jesus offers his prayer when his disciples ask him to teach them to pray. He doesn't give them a technique, though we will discuss some of those below. He gives them an attitude of prayer, and out of that attitude an acknowledgement of relationship, and in that relationship the things for which we ought to pray. It is a model; it is not meant to be the whole thing. We pray in the context of our lives. But this prayer gives us the wisdom of a framework in which to form our own prayer to our loving Abba.

The Leisure of Prayer

It may sound obvious, but what is required in prayer is setting aside time. That in itself is countercultural. We live in a world where busyness is a virtue. We need to recover the value of leisure in our busy society. I'm not just talking about how we spend our free time. Our culture tells us that our jobs should be our first priority. Our culture wants us to be consumers second and producers first. We live in a world where work consumes our lives. But our work should enhance our lives. The best work uses our talents for the greater good.

By the same token, leisure isn't just the need for rest so we can work more. In the 1950s, the Christian philosopher Josef Pieper critiqued our modern attitudes toward work and leisure.

> Leisure, it must be understood, is a mental and spiritual attitude—it is not simply the result of external factors, it is not the inevitable result of spare time, a holiday, a week-end or a vacation. It is, in the first place, an attitude of mind, a condition of the soul, and as such utterly contrary to the ideal of. . . work as activity, as toil, as a social function.[3]

Leisure as a frame of mind is a prerequisite of prayer. Leisure invites us to lay aside busyness and open our mind and soul to be receptive, rather than always active. Time spent in leisure isn't just an interruption in our work, but rather an essential element that enhances our lives, a time in which we can be present to God.

Silence and Solitude

When I stood in the Judean wilderness as part of my Holy Land pilgrimage, I was struck by the silence. I live in a city of millions of people. Even when I'm outside before dawn walking my dog, Mr. Jack, I hear cars in the distance, the low hum of the freeway in the background, and an occasional

---

3. Pieper, *Leisure*, 40.

helicopter. Out there in the wilderness there was sheer silence. I stood in the leisure of those moments by myself as dawn broke, looking across the seemingly endless hills. I allowed myself to be in the presence of God. The Judean wilderness was where Jesus went after his baptism to experience his "vision quest." Here, too, early Christian hermits, the fathers and mothers of the desert, went off to pray and experience the near presence of God. Jesus and his disciples often went to a place apart from the busyness of ministry, to refresh themselves, to re-focus, and to be renewed. What is it about a place of silence and solitude that helps us to pray? First, it's the leisure time itself, but most importantly it's the possibility of leaving aside the distractions that so often get in our way, or maybe the distractions we invite to keep us away from our deepest selves or from the possibility of an encounter with the "waking God" who "may draw us out to where we can never return," as Annie Dillard warns. Allowing ourselves the leisure of silence and solitude in prayer gives us an openness to be in God's presence without needing words, without an agenda. The wisdom of the Bible invites us into the silence. "Be still and know that I am God," says the psalmist. The Hebrew word we translate as "be still" here means to release, to let go and realize who is in charge. That's the attitude for contemplation of God. We release our need to be in control even of the experience of prayer. We don't set the agenda.

In my congregation, during our nighttime prayer service on Sundays called Compline, we often hear that verse read before we are invited into a brief time of silence and interior solitude. The cathedral is dark, apart from the glow of candles. The leader asks us to experience the words of the psalm:

Be still and know that I am God.
Be still and know that I am.
Be still and know.
Be still.
Be.

Stillness is an attitude of the heart and mind. We could be in the middle of the wilderness and not be away from noise or people. The external environment, whether in the Judean wilderness, out in the middle of a pine forest, or even our own backyard, helps us to encounter stillness, but it isn't the thing in itself. We have to consciously put aside what's going on at work or home. We have to place in the hands of God all the people we love or who it is challenging to love while we enter silence, solitude, and stillness. All those things and people will be there when we get back to our daily concerns. Just for a time, just in this moment, enter the place of stillness and "be."

Fixed Hour Prayer

A way of prayer I find most useful is fixed hour prayer, or what is also called the "liturgy of the hours" or the "divine office." This type of prayer happens at fixed hours of the day: morning, noon, and evening. Or it can be as simple as one time of day—for most people that's morning. This prayer emerges from the experience of monastic communities who would rise early to pray together and then at set hours of the day would come back together to pray.

Fixed hour prayer can be a fruitful experience for personal prayer as well. It is based on a set format using the Psalms as the foundation and then other readings of Scripture along with prayers. Forms for fixed hour prayer can be found on the internet or in the Book of Common Prayer from the Episcopal Church, for example. When you have a prayer book or electronic resource for this sort of prayer it takes you through a particular format for a particular day of the week and a season of the Church year. Fixed hour prayer, I find, is the best way to maintain a consistent regimen of daily prayer practice. The set order of this type of prayer allows me to just show up. I don't have to create an experience. There can be days when I'm totally immersed in the experience of praying the daily psalms and the readings speak right to me. I may remember the needs of the world, family, and friends and feel really close to God. Then there are other days when I practice the discipline of praying morning or evening prayer and there isn't anything about it that really grabs me. It seems dry, but I just show up. I am faithful to my practice.

Lectio Divina

Another way of praying with the Bible invites us to look at a single passage of Scripture and ruminate on it. "Ruminating" is the word medieval monks used when they talked about *lectio divina*, or divine reading, where we take a passage and read it over again with a different focus each time. Rumination is what a cow does by chewing its cud and chewing it over again. We repeatedly ingest God's word to us through the Scriptures through the practice of *lectio divina*.

There are four traditional phases in the practice of *lectio divina*, each preceded by reading the same passage. The first step is reading, or *lectio*: prayerfully and slowly allowing words or phrases to jump out at us. The second step is *meditatio*, or meditation, where we read the passage again and linger over those specific words or phrases that jumped out at us the first time, staying with the passage for as long as we wish. The third step, *oratio*, or praying with the passage, invites us to offer to God those thoughts the passage has evoked in us. This is prayer from our hearts. What do you want to say to God in response to what you have read? The fourth and final step, *contemplatio*—contemplation—asks us to read the passage a final time, and then to sit with it in the presence of God in silence, allowing God to speak to our hearts.

If you want to experiment with this type of prayer exercise, I suggest you use a brief reading that you can chew on over and over again. You might use, for example, the passage we discussed earlier from Mark's Gospel in which Jesus begins his public ministry. "Jesus came into Galilee announcing God's good news, saying, 'Now is the time! Here comes God's kingdom! Change your hearts and lives, and trust this good news!'" (Mark 1:14b–15, CEB) There are no hard and fast rules about the time this takes or what passage of Scripture you use. Just allow the steps to be a framework. The key is meeting God in the pages of the Bible speaking directly to you. Don't let the form get in the way of the encounter.

Imagination Prayer

A prayer form making use of our imaginations was made popular by Ignatius of Loyola, founder of the Jesuit religious order in the sixteenth century. Ignatius encourages us to take a story from the Gospels and let our imagination of the scene run wild. This method of praying with the Bible only works with a story, and with the Gospels in particular. The purpose of this method of prayer is to make Jesus come alive for you and to allow Jesus to speak through the story and through your imagination.

First, read the story and consider the details. Next, set the scene in your mind's eye. Let your senses work. What is the weather like? Is it cool or warm, rainy or sunny? You decide. This is not about the history of the event as much as your interaction with Jesus as he meets you in the story. Then consider who is there. Is there a crowd? Are there only a few people? What does Jesus look like? How does his voice sound? What do you see? Does the story in the Gospel involve water or desert? What other sounds do you hear? What do you smell? Can you taste anything in this story?

Once you have the scene composed in your mind, think about who you are. Are you an observer, part of a crowd? Are you one of the disciples? What is your perspective? Are you far away from the action or nearby? How do you feel—afraid, excited? In a way you have created a sort of movie of the story in your mind of which you are the director. Now allow the film to play out. Live the narrative in your imagination. What happens next? You can even allow other elements to be part of the scene that don't appear in the Gospel text. Simply remember that this is meant to draw you closer to Jesus.

The point of this prayer method is to open up the creative element of our brain in prayer. What is it that you notice that you hadn't noticed before about the story? What are you learning from it? What is Jesus asking you to do? What is he inviting you to see? Imaginative prayer also opens up the possibility for God to move past any barriers we normally may put up through our rational mind and allow elements to emerge from our subconscious self that might not be able to emerge otherwise. When you begin prayer in this way, invite Jesus to guide you through a particular event recorded in the Gospels. Ask him what he would have you learn from this story. How can you be a better disciple? Then as you close your prayer time, I suggest you might conclude with a well-known prayer from the thirteenth-century bishop Richard of Chichester:

Thanks be to you, our Lord Jesus Christ,
for all the benefits which you have given us,
for all the pains and insults which you have borne for us.
Most merciful Redeemer, Friend and Brother,
may we know you more clearly,
love you more dearly,
and follow you more nearly, day by day.

Stewardship of Our Time, Talent, and Treasure

How do we use all we have all the time as Christians? This question not only addresses how we manage our lives, but also how we share what we have. We use our talents and gifts in our work lives, but we have other talents we don't use in this way. What are our talents? What have we been given that we may not use and might begin to use? How can we use our talents and gifts to serve the Body of Christ and the wider world? These are questions we need to spend time thinking about. One way we can start to answer these questions is to see where there are needs in our congregations and in our wider communities. Can we be the people who can address those needs?

Spiritual writer Frederick Buechner says, "The place God calls you to is the place where your deep gladness and the world's deep hunger meet." Perhaps the first step in practicing this element of the Christian life is to take stock of what we have been given. What are our untapped inner resources or talents? What are we really good at that can serve the world's deep hunger? It might not be something spectacular, it might be mundane, but it is the way we can share what we have and who we are to heal a hole in the world.

I am a pretty good cook. I also have learned to can preserves, jams, and chutneys. I've found out I'm pretty good at it. The past few years, I've found produce in season and, over several months, canned all that beautiful fresh bounty. My congregation has a food pantry where we give away groceries to folks in need. Just before Christmas, I take all the jars I have made over the year and I offer them for sale after our Sunday services. The proceeds go to help defray costs for our food pantry. I am amazed that they sell out and people want more after they are all gone. Never underestimate your ability to offer a small thing and never underestimate what God can do with what you offer.

Money is another area many of us have difficulty with. If we as Christians want to place all our life under the Lordship of Jesus, that includes our finances. One of the greatest ways we can get an objective view of our priorities is by looking at the annual reports of our credit cards and checkbooks. Several years ago, I worked for a wonderful bishop of the Episcopal Church, Fred Borsch. He often said that in the days when Europe was being converted to Christianity warriors would hold up their swords in the right hand as they went into the water to be baptized. They didn't want to have to give up fighting so they thought they could get everything baptized except their sword arm. Bishop Borsch went on to say that in our society as we go into the water of baptism we hold up our wallets.

What portion of our financial resources will we commit to help those in need? What percentage of our financial resources will we share with our congregation? In the Old Testament, and still among many Christians today, the tithe—10 percent of our income—is held up as a standard of giving. I think that level of sacrificial giving is a good one, but I don't think there can be a hard and fast rule. Each of us knows the context of our own lives and financial situations. Some of us are unable to meet that goal; others of us will be able to give more. But we all need to reflect on how we use our finances to serve the kingdom of God, especially as part of the work of our congregations. In our culture, what we have is usually monetized, so sharing our money is an essential way we give to our brothers and sisters in Christ and to the needy. It's a key component of what it means to be disciples of Jesus Christ.

Food, Fasting, and Feasting

We live in a food-obsessed culture—what we eat, how we eat, when we eat it. We live in a culture where fast food restaurants are everywhere and we tend to "grab and go." Maybe we even eat in our cars on the way to the next thing in our busy lives. It often is a solitary activity. At the same time, we're surrounded by "food porn" ranging from billboards for fast food to exquisite presentations of gourmet dishes by master chefs making use of exotic ingredients. We live in a nation where we are inundated by food and images of food. We have an overabundance and we wind up throwing a lot of it away. At the same time many of our inner cities are food deserts where good nutrition is not readily available. In our nation and around the world vast numbers of people go hungry every day.

We need to think about Christian practices around food. I have had to ask myself some basic questions about where my food comes from, the cost of food, and the nutritional value of food. Choosing food grown without pesticides is a good place to start. Limiting how much meat I eat, and thinking about the conditions in which animals are raised or the working conditions of people who bring food to my table are others. What about the amount of resources it takes to raise animals for meat production? By raising these questions, I don't mean to induce guilt—that's counter-productive—but rather to make us examine our buying choices.

Also, I try to eat meals with other people whenever I can. If you live with other people, how often do you eat together? This is a particularly good question for families. We have allowed our busy schedules to dictate how we relate to one another. Making a family meal at least a couple of nights a week is a countercultural Christian practice.

Going without food, fasting, or abstaining from certain foods like meat on certain days are ancient practices in the Jewish and Christian traditions. First, in our culture, being mindful of what we consume and limiting it on certain days or times helps us realize our dependence on God and one another for what we have. Fasting is a form of prayer. When I experience physical hunger during a fast, I am reminded of why I'm doing it. It's a spiritual practice calling me to remember the presence of God and to focus my attention outside of my physical needs.

Fasting raises my consciousness about injustice as well. I am in solidarity with those who have no choice about whether they will eat today; even in our own country there are those who do not have enough food, or have little access to healthy food. My fasting can help me find ways I can help those who are hungry. When I'm directed to see injustice I'm called to penitence. Fasting becomes a way of asking God to redirect our hearts and minds away from self-concern and toward other people.

At the same time, there are days when we should feast with friends and family and the community of the church. Our bodies are God's gift to us and it's in our bodies that we celebrate and enjoy the wonderful gifts of God's creation. Food and drink shared with other people is one of the greatest joys in life. And part of feasting is the preparation of the food. For me, preparing a meal to share is an offering of love. The cooking itself is a spiritual practice. You may not find it so wonderful, and if you don't, there are creative ways to feast together even with simple things spread out on a table with other people gathered around. It's through these celebrations that we can come to know one another more deeply, and meet our Lord who meets us at table as an unseen guest.

Simplicity

Several years ago I came across an online video titled "The Story of Stuff." It outlines the cycle of production, purchasing, and disposal of the stuff we use and accumulate. It's an eye-opening look not only at our over-consumption, but at the tremendous waste and environmental damage it produces. Our American culture values buying and owning things as signs of identity and self-worth. The culture of consumption feeds us lies about who we are and where we find our worth.

Having what we need is certainly a good thing, but the practice of simplicity helps us prioritize our needs and curb our acquisitive desires to always have more, which our culture communicates to us on a daily basis. Simplicity is about taking an inventory of what we have and asking ourselves if we need it. Am I using it? Why am I keeping it? Could somebody else use it? How do I dispose of what I don't need? How is my consumption impacting the planet? These are all profoundly spiritual questions. From the very beginning the human vocation was to make good use of the earth's resources and to care for them as well.

Spiritual writer Esther De Waal talks about a specific practice to help ground us in simplicity of life based on being mindful of our relationship with possessions and even our own bodies. All we have is not ultimately ours. What we have will be left behind when we return to our creator. De Waal invites us to look around and name each thing we see. Start with that brand new flat screen TV and say to ourselves, "Not mine, just on temporary loan." Then maybe the armchair we are sitting in, "Not mine, just on temporary loan." Then once we've gone through the inventory of our stuff, we look at our bodies, our hands, our eyes, our ears, our feet and say, "Not mine, just on temporary loan." As we go through this exercise we can see that maybe we need to reorient our priorities about the "stuff" we have, since ultimately it really is only on loan.

At the same time, the things we have are meant to give us enjoyment. It may be the case that if we declutter our lives we will take greater joy and care of the things we have. It may influence what we purchase, as well. Simplicity is not about self-abasement. It's about valuing the things that we have and treating our possessions and our bodies as holy.

Communal Practices

As I've said, the practices of the spiritual life are interrelated, so although the practices I discuss as communal are grounded in our life together as Christians, they also have a personal dimension. Prayer, for example, can be both personal and corporate. Both are necessary to the Christian life. The communal aspect of Christianity is crucial. Jesus doesn't call us to be Lone Rangers but a band of pilgrims. What we experience in our personal and home lives can inform our experiences when we gather as the Church and the other way around.

Holy Time

We all have twenty-four hours in a day. We have the ability to use that time in a multitude of ways. We live in what might be called the world of work, where our culture continually asks us to sacrifice more and more of our time to our jobs so that economic life becomes more totalizing.

Christianity, as a countercultural movement, challenges us to see time in a different way. How can we structure our days, weeks, seasons, and years in a way that reflects who we are as God's beloved children? The answer to that question comes in the way the Christian tradition constructs times and seasons.

The Day

We've talked about fixed hour prayer that assumes the punctuation of our day by prayer in the morning, noontime, and evening. There also is a time of prayer before bedtime called Compline. Praying at these times joins Christians around the world in the communal prayer of the Church. It's incredible to think that my prayer is part of a global "wave." As others end their prayers in another part of the world, I am beginning mine so that the round of Christians praying is ceaseless.

The Week

Remember the creation stories from the book of Genesis we explored in chapter 2? God engages in creative work (not monotonous drudgery) for six days and then rests on the seventh day. Remember God also creates human beings in God's image, male and female. He invites us to make use of the resources of the earth and to preserve them for our benefit and for those who come after us. Work is a holy enterprise. Benedict in his Rule of Life for monks emphasizes prayer and work, leisure and labor to create balance in our lives.

The figure below indicates the rhythm of the week, culminating in Sunday, the first day of the week, sometimes called the "eighth day," because it's the first day of the week, the start of a whole new way of time-keeping, the beginning of the new creation. Thursday and Friday of any week also can be times when we acknowledge our Lord's suffering and death, and Saturday we acknowledge God's rest from the work of creation.

THE SPIRITUAL RHYTHM OF THE WEEK

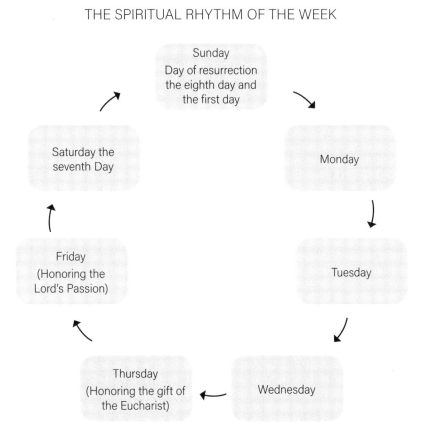

Six days a week we engage in work that hopefully makes us feel we are contributing to the life of the world in some way. Then we are invited to keep Sabbath. The Jewish tradition is much better about this than the Christian one. Yet Sabbath is part of our life as well. In fact it is part of the Ten Commandments.

Lauren Winner is a Christian convert from Judaism. Her insights are particularly instructive when it comes to Sabbath observance for Christians. She acknowledges that in the New Testament the observance of the law no longer binds Christians who have entered the new life in Christ for which the law prepared the way:

But there is something in the Jewish Sabbath that is absent from most Christian Sundays: a true cessation from the rhythms of work and world, a time wholly set apart, and, perhaps above all, a sense that the point of Shabbat, the orientation of Shabbat, is toward God. . . . The Sabbath has come back into fashion, even among the most secular of Americans, but the Sabbath we now embrace is a curious one. Articles abound extolling of treating yourself to a day of rest. . . Take a day off, the magazines urge their harried readers. Rest.

There might be something to celebrate in this revival of Sabbath, but is seems to me there are at least two flaws in the reasoning. First is what we might call capitalism's justification for Sabbath rest: resting one day a week makes you more productive during the other six. . . And while that may be true, rest for the sake of future productivity is at odds with the spirit of Shabbat.

We could call the second problem with the current Sabbath vogue the fallacy of the direct object. Whom is the contemporary Sabbath designed to honor? The Bible suggests. . . in observing Sabbath, one is giving a gift to God and imitating him.[4]

Winner's insights draw us deeply into the meaning of sanctifying the week as holy, both our labor and our leisure. It isn't meant to honor our economic structures or ourselves—that is idolatry (see the Ten Commandments again). It's meant for us to rest in our identity as created in the image of God and to honor and delight our creator with the joy of playfulness.

That brings me to the argument that Christians no longer observe the law. Yes, we have entered a new dimension as citizens of the new creation, but our observance of the Sabbath is equally holy, because we participate in a time beyond time, a new world order on the Sabbath, as we come together on the Lord's Day, to celebrate the resurrection—on Sunday rather than Saturday. We gather at the Lord's Table to share the food and drink of the heavenly banquet in Holy Communion and anticipate our

---

4. Winner, *Mudhouse Sabbath*, 12–13.

life in God's kingdom when it comes in its fullness. Unfortunately, the economic systems use our "freedom from the law" as a convenient means of further enslaving us in the world of total work. Jesus has a different idea in mind and we as his disciples should challenge the culture by Sabbath rest as an act of prophetic resistance.

Sabbath as resistance is echoed in a wonderful little book by the insightful Old Testament scholar Walter Brueggemann:.

> In our contemporary context of the rat race of anxiety, the celebration of Sabbath is an act of both resistance and alternative. It is resistance because it is a visible insistence that our lives are not defined by the production and consumption of commodity goods. Such an act of resistance requires enormous intentionality and communal reinforcement amid the barrage of seductive pressures from the insatiable insistences of the market, with its intrusion into every part of our life. . .
>
> But Sabbath is not only resistance. It is alternative. It is an alternative to the demanding, chattering, pervasive presence of advertising and its great liturgical claim of professional sports that devour all our "rest time."[5]

All the allures of our culture seek to make us busy even in our leisure and to work even when we are at rest. Having a "free day" doesn't mean we fill it with more busyness—that includes sports practice for our kids. One of the greatest witnesses to keeping Sabbath happens among Mormons. I have heard of parents who simply stand up to coaches and say, "Sunday is our Sabbath. What alternatives will you make for our children's schedules?" That's a countercultural witness from which we all can draw a lesson.

Seasons of the Year

The wisdom of the tradition gives us a whole cycle of the year as well as the week centered around the life of Christ and the two major festivals,

---

5. Brueggemann, *Sabbath as Resistance*, xiii–iv.

Easter as foremost, and secondarily Christmas—the latter of course having also been co-opted by the forces of the market economy. The figure
below outlines the rhythm of the church year.

SANCTIFYING THE CIRCLE OF THE YEAR

Triduum and Easter
Season to Pentecost
Related to the
Spring Equinox

Ordinary time of the
year after Pentecost
(variable length)

Lent

Advent

Season After
Epiphany
(variable length)

Christmas Season
through the Epiphany
Related to the Winter
Solstice

Notice that the two major feasts relate to the rhythms of the natural world. Advent and Christmas come at the darkest time of the year
in which we celebrate the festival of light coming into the world. Lent,
from the old German and English word meaning to lengthen—as in the
lengthening of the days—comes during spring, recalling new life born
from death. During Lent we prepare for that primary festival of the year,
Easter: the celebration of Jesus's death and resurrection. These seasons and

feasts keep us mindful of the central mysteries of our faith and we celebrate them in our common worship.

I mentioned fasting and feasting above as personal practices. These are ways we keep these seasons in our daily lives. Lent, and to a lesser extent Advent, are seasons of preparation where fasting and introspection are ways of preparation. The Christmas season (not just a day) and the Easter season are times of feasting.

There are other practices that can bring these feasts into our homes. Before Christmas, the Advent wreath is a great time-keeping device to count down to Christmas. Four candles are placed in a circle. Each week a candle is lit. Traditionally three are purple and one pink, which is used in the third week, often called "rejoicing" Sunday. At Easter, coloring eggs, a tradition in the wider culture, has deep symbolic meaning for Christians and is an excellent teaching tool for children. Colored eggs as a joyful sign of spring, the season of new and abundant life; a brand new life emerges out of the hard shell of the egg, like Jesus from the tomb on Easter morning.

There are all sorts of ways to remember and celebrate these seasons far beyond the scope of this book, both in the communal life of your congregation and in your home life. The main idea is that keeping holy time reminds us that we are citizens of another country, that we are freed from the constraints of the consumer culture because we are beloved children of God, no longer slaves of Pharaoh, and we can make present again those events in the life of Jesus that have made possible our lives as Christians in the world.

Worship

A natural segue from the church year is communal worship. While daily prayer practices ground us personally in our faith lives, worship grounds us as communities of Christians in our mission to the world. Particularly, the practice takes place on Sunday mornings. The chief act of communal worship on Sundays is the celebration of the Eucharist. I discussed that great sacrament in the previous chapter. Here, let's focus on the communal elements. When we gather as communities of faith on Sunday both the word and the sacrament are shared. First, we hear the word of Scripture proclaimed and then broken open for us through the sermon. What's key here is that we do this together. We are a community of disciples gathered as those first disciples were on Easter evening when the Lord stood in their midst and spoke to them. Whenever we gather together, Jesus promises he will be with us. Together we hear his voice speaking to us and that word is broken open for us in our own context. What does this word, spoken in this particular community, on this particular day, mean for us?

Then we go to the Table of the Lord. Remember the dramaturgy of celebrating this sacrament? We tell the story of what Jesus did on the night before he died while we actually do what he said to do. Together we do those very things Jesus did when he fed the five thousand, when he sat at table with his disciples at the last supper, and what he did in the little village of Emmaus when two were gathered there with him. He took bread, blessed it, broke it, and shared it. Then he took the cup of his blood and shared it. That's why the symbolism of the common cup is beautiful in sharing with one another.

Think of what you see in that moment. God's people, the Body of Christ, siblings of the same Father come together and receive the same food and drink side by side. We celebrate right now what the new creation banquet will be. In that sacramental moment we "re-member" Jesus—we make his body present through our bodies. Then we break up our gathering to go share what we have received with those we meet in our daily lives. That's the mission we are sent out to do after we have worshipped together.

There are other times of worship that are not focused on the Eucharist. We can come together for times of prayer and to hear the Scriptures. Daily morning or evening prayer are celebrated together in many places. We can gather in one another's homes for small groups and pray together and study the Scriptures. Jesus's promise still remains true for us that whenever two or three gather together in his name, there he is in the midst of us, and every time I know he continues to bless us with those Easter words, "Peace be with you." God's well-being, God's right relationship, God's loving forgiveness be with you.

Hospitality

In my congregation we sometimes call the coffee hour or the reception after worship "the eighth sacrament." We say it jokingly, as if it's as important as what we have just done at the Lord's Table. Yet, in a way it is a continuation of what we have just done. At the Lord's Table, Jesus offers us his body and blood as the free gift of new life. Remember in Luke's Easter story, when Jesus and the two disciples reach Emmaus, how Jesus acts as if he will continue walking? He doesn't presume on the hospitality of his friends, but they offer it to him. "Stay with us, because it is almost evening and the day is now nearly over" (Luke 24:29). It's only then that he joins them at table, but strangely, he becomes the host of the meal, taking the bread, and sharing it. It's in that moment that they recognize him.

It's the same with us. Jesus shares his meal and invites us to share hospitality with one another. Hospitality and Eucharist go together. We as Christians gather together and share meals with one another; we feast together. One thing I've noticed is that regardless of the denomination or the differences we Christians have, one thing we like to do is get together for a meal. That's what Jesus did so often. Hospitality was a hallmark of his ministry. We see him again and again sitting down at table with all sorts of people. That's what he wants us to do. He asks us to share our abundance with each other and especially with the stranger in our midst. That is a transformative spiritual practice because we meet one another as Christians by breaking our bread. I think that experience makes it easier to open ourselves to one another as well.

The hospitality of the Lord's Table gets lived out also when communities of Christians share their bread with those who have little or nothing to eat. Food banks providing groceries to people who are in need, or meals programs for the elderly or helping to feed the homeless, are all core spiritual practices in the Christian life and they are directly connected with the Eucharist. What we perform at the Lord's Table demonstrates that we all receive what we have from God's abundance, so we share that with those in need around us.

Hospitality shared in the community of the Church or with small groups of Christians also helps us learn how we should live our daily lives.

Are there ways we can open our homes in hospitality to others? Can we share meals with friends, or even possibly invite those who are strangers or outsiders in? How is Jesus calling us to extend the hospitality of the Lord's Table into our homes? How can our homes be little outposts of God's kingdom extending neighborliness to those around us? I ask these questions not as if there is a single answer for everyone in every place, but as starting points for all of us to think where we might extend the abundance of the love, generosity, and hospitality of the same God who created us and gives us abundance to share with others.

Missional Practices

Missional practices are those acts we do either on our own or through our churches to reach out to our neighborhoods and wider communities. The goal of these practices is to create demonstration projects of the new creation in ways large and small. In the Episcopal Church, we have a succinct mission statement in the Book of Common Prayer that I think is transferrable to all Christians: "To restore all people to unity with God in Christ." Isn't that really God's dream? That leads me to a fundamental question about missional practices. We sometimes get caught up in what we do, especially as churches, and we sometimes lose track of why we do them. If we keep the church's mission at the forefront of our minds as the basis for what we do, then we can have a clearer vision of whether the things we do reflect that mission.

Evangelism

Evangelism, as we discussed earlier in this book, is all about letting people know about the good news of the Jesus movement. As individuals and as communities we have the opportunity to share our faith with those who have not yet heard it. As we know, there are lots of people who have distorted ideas about what Christianity is about. Our job as Christians is to proclaim by example and word (notice which one I put first) the good news of God in Christ. If people come to know that you have a faith that makes a difference in your life, they are going to be curious about it. Evangelism as a Christian practice does not mean going door to door asking people if they are saved. It simply means being willing to share your faith when the time is right and not in a way that conveys superiority. It also means inviting others to speak and share their story with you.

Acts of Mercy

Congregations are the best location for the practice of mercy. Lots of congregations or other church structures have been doing this since the beginning of Christianity—hospitals, social service agencies, orphanages, and other institutions often have their basis in missions of churches or religious orders. All of these are examples of showing mercy, that is, seeing a need in the world and offering to meet it in some way based on the Church's mission. When we care for those in need, we are living out the mission of Jesus to restore God's peace to the world. Healing and helping wounded people is a means of restoring them to wholeness and giving them a sense of their own inherent dignity as created in the image of God.

Individual congregations have all sorts of mercy ministries: food pantries, homeless shelters, clinics, day care, and tutoring to name just a few. These ministries work because individual Christians and other people of goodwill engage in the practice of mercy. Our Lord's greatest challenge to us is to see him in the distressing disguise of those in need. Famously, in the twenty-fifth chapter of Matthew's Gospel, Jesus reminds us that whenever we feed the hungry, give drink to the thirsty, clothe the naked, visit prisoners we are doing it to him.

Peace and Social Justice Actions

While works of mercy make a direct impact on the needs of people who often are poor and marginalized, peace and justice actions are those seeking to effect social and structural change. These practices include individual acts of writing to governmental officials to make your position known on political issues. It can also be direct actions of protest and resistance to situations where the society has turned away from what we know to be God's hope for us. These can include protests against gun violence or in favor of more just wages. The list of possible social justice actions is long. It is crucial, though, for Christians to realize that these actions are done not because they represent any one political party or affiliation, but because they are the logical living out of the Gospel. Our question should not be "What would Jesus do?" regarding any particular question of injustice, but rather, "What *is* Jesus asking us to do in this particular time and place?" As I have said, we aren't looking to a prophet in the past. We serve a risen Lord with us in the present whose Holy Spirit is guiding us into the future.

Many of the social issues the Church must engage are complex and multifaceted. That is why it's crucial for Christians to engage in mutual discernment and conversation as part of our engagement in political action. Even though action for social justice is complex, we should not avoid it. At the very heart of the Gospel and the prophetic tradition is the call to engage social structures and speak out against injustice in which the principalities and powers of this world seek to crush the least, the last, and the lost of society through injustice in the economic, social, military, and political spheres.

I once had a well-meaning couple leave our church because we took stands on political issues. They believed the Church should only be about forming Christian values within individual hearts. They asked if I could recommend a church that felt as they did. While I might have been able to find one, I did not recommend it, because I believe the social dimension of Christianity is so central to its mission that a church that doesn't speak out to help transform the world is one that has lost its way. Our job is claiming the cosmos for the kingdom of God and that means standing against the forces of the dark lord wherever we find them. We are not always successful and we are not always courageous enough in making our voices heard, but speak and act we must.

To be a Christian is to be one in the world. We cannot escape it. To help to make positive material changes in the order of society is part of our mission to restore all people to unity with each other, as well as God in Christ. To engage in acts of mercy and justice is to serve Christ. To daily practice our Christian vocation is to follow Christ. To engage our bodies and minds in prayer is to worship Christ. We engage all these practices in and through the world God loves so much—the world God entered in the real flesh and blood of our living Lord.

Questions for Reflection

1. The wisdom of St. Benedict and the monastic tradition teaches us about balancing our life. Today there is a lot of discussion about maintaining a work/life balance. How can we use the tools of the spiritual practices to help us?

2. Do you pray? What are your prayer practices? Are there any we have discussed in this chapter you find appealing?

3. Observing Sabbath is not easy. Why do you think that is? How is Sabbath-keeping countercultural?

4. Have you engaged in consistent practices that have become habits? What have they been? Have they changed you, and in what ways? How might spiritual practices transform your life?

10

Home

Toward the beginning of his Gospel, Matthew tells the tale of sages searching the night sky in a far-off land. Matthew tells us they show up in Jerusalem and inquire of the wicked King Herod where the king of the Jews was to be born. They had seen his star at its rising and came to pay him homage. What made those ancient wise seekers look up at the night sky in the first place? Were they looking for celestial pings? Mathew's telling of the story reminds me that God calls us wherever we are, using whatever way we will hear or see to draw us to journey home, whether we come from afar or nearby.

At the end of Matthew's story, these wise stargazers offer costly gifts to the infant Jesus. Then they go "home by another way." That's a strange line, but effective. They are changed by their pilgrimage and by meeting the one they travelled to find, following his star. Where was home for them? Home would never be the same because they still were on a journey; so are we.

I began this book looking at stars. When we look at the night sky like those ancient travelers, we are compelled to connect with something, someone beyond ourselves. This book has been about that journey, about how the creator of all things has sent pings into the universe attempting to connect with wandering seekers like you and like me.

I've told the story of how this God has come among us, leading us to freedom like following the bright North Star. Maybe you are open to continue exploring. Maybe you have decided to follow Jesus, the Risen One. The book of Revelation and the Second Letter of Peter both refer to him as the Morning Star, the planet Venus in the sky rising before dawn. We follow him through the darkness of this world with hope that day will break in its fullness. That's the hope I have tried to convey as we make our journey home.

There will come a time when you and I will breathe our last. The assurance of the Christian message is that there is more than that for us. When we leave this dimension, we will enter another that the Bible calls heaven or paradise. I imagine that right now, on the other side of the veil of this world, the other dimension exists with all those we have loved and lost already living in a greater light and on a distant shore. And I think of all of them urging us on.

The author of the Second Letter to Timothy (attributed to the apostle Paul) writes this:

> I have fought the good fight, finished the race, and kept the faith. At last the champion's wreath that is awarded for righteousness is waiting for me. The Lord, who is the righteous judge, is going to give it to me on that day. He's giving it not only to me but also to all those who have set their heart on waiting for his appearance.[1]

We all are in that race. Think of those who have gone before us as we enter that place of larger life and as we receive the champion's wreath.

I had a dream once—one of those dreams that stay with you and you can't shake. It is very early in the morning just as darkness fades into dim light. I am being hurried along by a few guys I don't know, but for some reason I think it's all okay. For some reason I know they're fishermen. We wind around some rocks leading down to the water. There's a fishing boat

---

1. 2 Tim. 4:7–8, CEB.

there and they ask me to get in. "Hurry up," they say, "we don't have much time." They are looking forward to something ahead. We set off and soon the mist that has been over the water begins to break up and I see a shore ahead of me and there among crowds of people I make out faces of those I have known and loved, all who have already gone from this present existence. I'm filled with joy at seeing them out ahead of me. That's how the dream ends. It's a dream that gives me assurance of what awaits on the other side of the veil.

But the paradise we look forward to isn't the only future. The New Testament looks forward to a whole new world. This world, this cosmos, will be transformed. In the last book of the Bible, Revelation or the Apocalypse (a word meaning the unveiling), the mystic visionary John sees the new order being joined with this one. An angel declares,

> The kingdom of the world has become
> the kingdom of our Lord and his Christ,
> and he will rule forever and always.[2]

Our ultimate hope is not going to heaven when we die, but something more wonderful. The cosmos we live in now will no longer be the haunt of the dark lord and the powers of evil, but it will be transformed. All those who have gone before us are waiting for the transformation of this creation. We will not be snatched out to go somewhere else.

There are some Christians who believe there will be a "rapture" in which all those who are saved will be taken out of this world and the ultimate end of our present cosmos will be destruction. That understanding of God's future is relatively modern, emerging out of certain parts of the Evangelical tradition. It became especially popular in the United States beginning in the nineteenth century. It does not appear in the Christian tradition before that time. The folks who believe in the rapture selectively use texts to bolster their position, but the Bible itself does not support it.

If you hold a rapture view of the end of the world your vision of this world is radically different from the one I have proposed in this

---

2. Rev. 11:15b, ceb.

book and what the Christian tradition has imagined. The mission of Christians from the rapture point of view is to "save" as many people from the coming destruction as possible. To get them ready for the great escape. For them, whatever we do in this world may be helpful in making us more holy for the future, but in itself our work has no permanent value in this world.

But if we believe that God's ultimate hope is to save us for this world, rather than from it, our perspective becomes very different. Everything we do in this world as pioneers of the new creation will have lasting and eternal significance. We are building now for the world of the future. The good news is that you and I will be part of it and not just as "souls, but as wholes." The risen body of Jesus is the first born of a whole new creation. There will be a "great getting up morning" as the old spiritual puts it, and we will see it in our bodies, renewed bodies like that of Jesus, but real bodies nonetheless. Paul the apostle insists on this hope:

> But in fact Christ has been raised from the dead. He's the first crop of the harvest of those who have died. Since death came through a human being, the resurrection of the dead came through one too. In the same way that everyone dies in Adam, so also everyone will be given life in Christ. Each event will happen in the right order: Christ, the first crop of the harvest, then those who belong to Christ at his coming, and then the end, when Christ hands over the kingdom to God the Father, when he brings every form of rule, every authority and power to an end. . . As a result of all this, my loved brothers and sisters, you must stand firm, unshakable, excelling in the work of the Lord as always, because you know that your labor isn't going to be for nothing in the Lord.[3]

We don't always focus on this vision. We tend to focus on our souls getting to heaven, but that's not God's last word. The good news is better than that. Bishop Tom Wright encourages us when he says:

---

3. 1 Cor. 15:20–24, 58, CEB.

What you do in the Lord is not in vain. You are not oiling the wheels of a machine that's about to roll over a cliff. You are not restoring a great painting that's shortly going to be thrown on the fire. You are not planting roses in a garden that's about to be dug up for a building site. You are—strange as it may seem, almost as hard to believe as the resurrection itself—accomplishing something that will become in due course part of God's new world. . . God's recreation of his wonderful world, which began with the resurrection of Jesus and continues mysteriously as God's people live in the risen Christ and in the power of his Spirit, means that what we do in Christ and by the Spirit in the present is not wasted. It will last all the way into God's new world. In fact it will be enhanced there.[4]

As we come to the end of this journey together, our greater pilgrimage continues. All the practices we engage in throughout our lives will not be in vain. Your life is not in vain. Your hope will not be in vain.

At our best, we Christians give voice to the greatest aspirations of humanity. Humans have always been trying to find a way home. Our often utopian visions for our communities and our cities embody that hope for a place where we are in right relationship with one another and with God. We want to have balance between human communities and the natural world. In the 1830s, the city of Chicago adopted a motto, "*urbs in horto*"—"a city in a garden." The vision was to develop a city integrating the natural world with human culture, community, and commerce. That's just one small example of our human vision. And yet, as we know, Chicago, like all our cities, falls short of its dream. Crime, poverty, and racial issues have been persistent problems. Yet, "*urbs in horto*" is what we dream of as the ideal of human flourishing.

The Bible begins in a garden and it ends in a city that embodies the dream of "*urbs in horto*." John the mystic saw the vision of the new world coming into being, the heavenly city joining with the earthly one:

> Then I saw a new heaven and a new earth, for the former heaven and the former earth had passed away, and the sea was no more. I

---

4. Wright, *Surprised by Hope*, 208–9.

saw the holy city, New Jerusalem, coming down out of heaven from God, made ready as a bride beautifully dressed for her husband. I heard a loud voice from the throne say, "Look! God's dwelling is here with humankind. He will dwell with them, and they will be his peoples. God himself will be with them as their God. He will wipe away every tear from their eyes. Death will be no more. There will be no mourning, crying, or pain anymore, for the former things have passed away." Then the one seated on the throne said, "Look! I'm making all things new." . . . I didn't see a temple in the city, because its temple is the Lord God Almighty and the Lamb. The city doesn't need the sun or the moon to shine on it, because God's glory is its light, and its lamp is the Lamb. The nations will walk by its light, and the kings of the earth will bring their glory into it. Its gates will never be shut by day, and there will be no night there. They will bring the glory and honor of the nations into it. Nothing unclean will ever enter it, nor anyone who does what is vile and deceitful, but only those who are registered in the Lamb's scroll of life. Then the angel showed me the river of life-giving water, shining like crystal, flowing from the throne of God and the Lamb through the middle of the city's main street. On each side of the river is the tree of life, which produces twelve crops of fruit, bearing its fruit each month. The tree's leaves are for the healing of the nations. There will no longer be any curse. The throne of God and the Lamb will be in it, and his servants will worship him. They will see his face, and his name will be on their foreheads. Night will be no more. They won't need the light of a lamp or the light of the sun, for the Lord God will shine on them, and they will rule forever and always.[5]

The vision is of the garden again, but one in the midst of the city. God's dream finally coming in its fullness embodies both the beauty of creation and the work of God's divine image-bearers—human beings. I cannot say how all this will come about, but I have faith and hope in the future. C. S. Lewis's words come once again to mind:

---

5. Rev. 21:1–5a, 21:22–22:5, CEB.

At present we are on the outside of the world, the wrong side of the door. We discern the freshness and purity of morning, but they do not make us fresh and pure. We cannot mingle with the splendors we see. But all the leaves of the New Testament are rustling with the rumor that it will not always be so. Some day, God willing, we shall get in.[6]

We pilgrims continue to follow the Pole Star, the risen Lord who leads us home. And in the meantime, let's give voice to the dream of humanity, the hope of all those created in the image of God who have a God-shaped hole in their hearts trying to find the way home. Like Harriet Tubman, can we lead wanderers onto the path of life? Can we build for the kingdom? Can we create signposts to show the way? Can we be light to the world? That's our mission for the road ahead.

In 1971 the Armenian Patriarch of Jerusalem commissioned an archeological dig in a portion of the Church of the Holy Sepulcher. Archeologists came across ancient stones dating to the time of Queen Helena, in the fourth century. She had the temple of Venus destroyed, which the emperor Hadrian had built over the site in the late first century, in order to build the first Christian church there. On one of those first-century stones discovered in the excavation was a crude carving depicting a little ship typical of those used to travel the Mediterranean in those days. The ship is storm-tossed; the mast of the ship appears to be broken. Below it was scratched the inscription "*Domine Ivimus*"—"Lord, we came."

It may well be that a group of pilgrims in the first or second century travelled to the place of Jesus's crucifixion, burial, and resurrection. Perhaps they etched their carving into the temple built over the site and left their mark of faith, a touching reminder that we are all pilgrims who have travelled this road. Maybe they wanted us to know that, despite the rigors of the journey, they still had arrived. They offered their carving as a prayer left in stone. I also imagine they wryly knew that, though the temple of the goddess Venus stood there, the true Morning Star was not

---

6. Lewis, *The Weight of Glory*, 43.

the planet Venus rising, but the risen Jesus who had led them to that place, and they sought to do him honor.

When I came as a pilgrim to the place of our Lord's crucifixion, burial, and resurrection I said that little prayer offered by that band of pilgrims nearly two thousand years ago, "Lord, I came." I also realized that I was at the place where my Lord shared in my death and in my burial and in the resurrection I will one day share with him. So it is for all of us. When we come to that day, when we take our last breath, Christ will make room by his tomb for us. He will call us by name in the garden early in the morning as the sun is rising. And after our journey's end, we, too, will joyfully proclaim, "Domine Ivimus." Lord, we came.

Questions for Reflection

1. Some Christians believe in a "rapture" at the end of time, others believe in the transformation of this creation. What practical impact might those two views have on the way we live in the world?

2. How can Christians create signs or "sacraments" of God's hope for the world in our daily lives? How does the vision of a city and a garden reflect that hope?

3. At the end of this pilgrimage together, what insights, if any, have you gained for your spiritual life?

WORKS CITED

Alter, Robert. *Genesis: Translation and Commentary.* New York: W. W. Norton and Co., 1996.

Anderson, Carol, and Peter Summers. *Who Do You Say That I Am?* Tunbridge Wells: Monarch, 1993.

Augustine. *Confessions.* Translated by Maria Boulding. New York: Random House, 1997.

Bauman, Zygmund. *Postmodern Ethics.* Oxford: Blackwell Publishers, 1993.

Borg, Marcus J., and John Dominic Crossan. *The Last Week: The Day by Day Account of Jesus' Final Week in Jerusalem.* San Francisco: HarperCollins, 2006.

Brown, Brené. *Daring Greatly.* New York: Penguin, 2012.

Brueggemann, Walter. *Sabbath as Resistance: Saying No to the Culture of Now.* Louisville, KY: Westminster John Knox Press, 2014.

Buber, Martin. *Good and Evil.* New York: Scribner, 1952.

Cahill, Thomas. *Desire of the Everlasting Hills: The World Before and After Jesus.* New York: Doubleday, 1999.

Capon, Robert Farrar. *Kingdom, Grace, Judgment: Paradox, Outrage, and Vindication in the Parables of Jesus.* Grand Rapids: Eerdmans, 2002.

Cottingham, John. *Why Believe.* New York: Continuum, 2009.

De Waal, Esther. *Living with Contradiction: Reflections on the Rule of St. Benedict.* New York: Harper and Row, 1989.

Dillard, Annie. *The Abundance: Narrative Essays Old and New.* New York: Harper, 2016.

DuBois, Constance Goddard. "Mythology of the Mission Indians." *The Journal of the American Folk-Lore Society*, Vol. XVII. No. 66, [1904]: 52–60.

Greenblatt, Stephen. *The Swerve: How the World Became Modern.* New York: W.W. Norton and Co., 2011.

Griffith-Jones, Robin. *The Four Witnesses: The Rebel, the Rabbi, the Chronicler, and the Mystic.* New York: HarperCollins, 2000.

Hawking, Stephen, and Leonard Mlodinow. *The Grand Design.* New York: Bantam Books, 2010.

Johnson, Luke Timothy. *Creed: What Christians Believe and Why It Matters.* New York: Doubleday, 2003.

———. *The Real Jesus: The Misguided Quest for the Historical Jesus and the Truth of the Traditional Gospels.* New York: HarperCollins, 1996.

Kenyon, Jane. *Collected Poems.* St. Paul, MN: Graywolf Press, 2005.

Lewis, C. S. "Mere Christianity." In *The Complete C. S. Lewis Signature Classics*, by C. S. Lewis, 1–178. New York: HarperCollins, 2002.

———. "The Weight of Glory." In *The Weight of Glory and Other Addresses*, by C. S. Lewis, 25–46. New York: HarperCollins, 1976.

Louth, Andrew, ed. *Genesis 1–11, Ancient Christian Commentary on Scripture, vol. 1.* Downers Grove, IL: Intervarsity Press, 2001.

Magonet, Jonathan. *A Rabbi Reads the Bible.* London: SCM Press, 2004.

Merritt, Jonathan. *Learning to Speak God from Scratch: Why Sacred Words Are Vanishing and How We Can Revive Them.* New York: Convergent Books, 2018.

Nayeri, Farah. "A Bright Window Into His Own Faith." *The New York Times*, October 3, 2018: C5.

Pew Research Center. "America's Changing Religious Landscape." May 12, 2015.

Pieper, Josef. *Leisure the Basis of Culture.* New York: Random House, 1963.

Porter, Anne. "Music." In *Living Things: Collected Poems.* Hanover, NH: Steerforth Press, 2006.

Sagoff, Mark. "Do We Consume Too Much?" *The Atlantic*, June 1997: digital edition.

Silberman, Neil Asher, and Israel Finkelstein. *The Bible Unearthed: Archeology's New Vision of Ancient Israel and the Origin of Its Sacred Texts.* New York: Touchstone, 2001.

Sohn, Rabbi Ruth H. *Does Abraham's Covenant Include Jewish Daughters?* (accessed January 2017).

Taylor, Charles. *A Secular Age.* Cambridge, MA: Harvard University Press, 2007.

Thomas, Dylan. *The Collected Poems of Dylan Thomas.* Edited by John Goodby. London: Weidenfeld & Nicolson, 2016.

Vogel, Arthur A. *Radical Christianity and the Flesh of Jesus.* Grand Rapids: Eerdmans, 1995.

Winner, Lauren F. *Mudhouse Sabbath: An Invitation to a Life of Spiritual Discipline.* Brewster, MA: Paraclete Press, 2003.

Winslow, Don. *The Power of the Dog.* New York: Alfred A. Knopf, 2005.

Wright, N. T. *Surprised by Hope: Rethinking Heaven, the Resurrection, and the Mission of the Church.* New York: HarperCollins, 2008.

———. "The Mission and Message of Jesus." In *The Meaning of Jesus: Two Visions*, by Marcus J. Borg and N.T. Wright. New York: HarperCollins e-books.

Zerubavel, Evator. *Ancestors and Relatives: Genealogy, Identity and Community.* New York: Oxford University Press, 2011.